OSPREY AIRCRAFT OF THE ACES • 83

Malta Spitfire Aces

SERIES EDITOR: TONY HOLMES

OSPREY AIRCRAFT OF THE ACES • 83

Malta Spitfire Aces

Steve Nichols

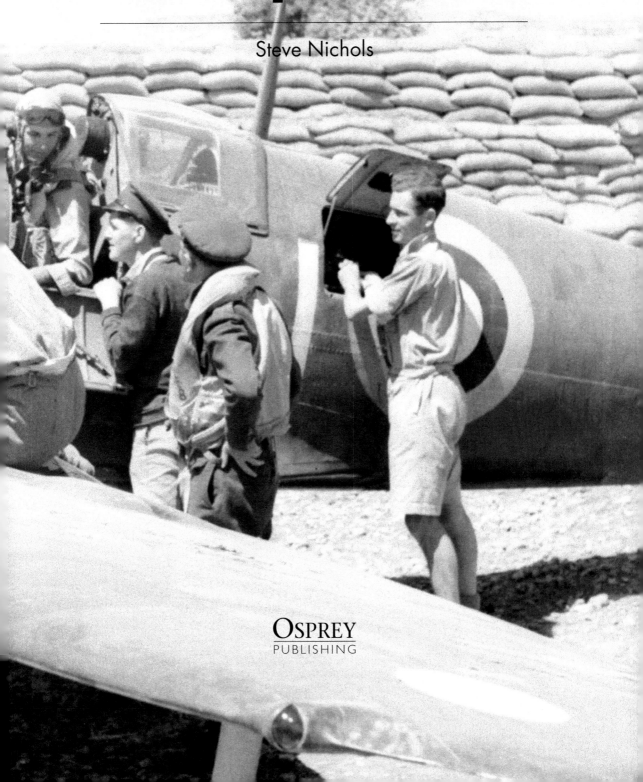

OSPREY
PUBLISHING

First published in Great Britain in 2008 by Osprey Publishing,
PO Box 883, Oxford, OX1 9PL, UK
PO Box 3985, New York, NY 10185-3985, USA
Email: info@ospreypublishing.com

Osprey Publishing is part of the Osprey Group.

Transferred to digital print on demand 2013

First published 2008
3rd impression 2010

Printed and bound by PrintOnDemand-Worldwide.com, Peterborough, UK

A CIP catalogue record for this book is available from the British Library

ISBN: 978 1 84603 305 6

Edited by Tony Holmes
Page design by Tony Truscott
Cover artwork by Mark Postlethwaite
Aircraft profiles by Steve Nichols
Scale drawings by Steve Nichols and Mark Styling
Index by Alan Rutter
Originated by United Graphic

The Woodland Trust
Osprey Publishing is supporting the Woodland Trust, the UK's leading woodland conservation charity, by
funding the dedication of trees.

www.ospreypublishing.com

Front Cover
On 27 July 1942, Canadian Sgt George Beurling fought his most famous aerial engagement in the
skies over the Mediterranean. He would emerge from the clash with both German and Italian fighters
as the leading Allied ace of the Malta siege.

At 0835 hrs on the 27th, nine Ju 88s, escorted by C.202s and Bf 109Fs, headed for Takali airfield
from their bases on the Italian island of Sicily. Eight Spitfire VCs from No 185 Sqn attempted to
intercept the enemy aircraft, but they were vectored onto the formation too late. Eight more Spitfire
VCs from No 126 Sqn pursued the Ju 88s after they had bombed Takali, although they in turn came
under attack from 13 C.202s of 20° Gruppo and 155° Gruppo. At this moment six Spitfire VCs from No
249 Sqn intervened. One of the British fighters – BR301 – was flown by Beurling, this machine having
emerged as his 'lucky' aircraft. It would eventually be credited with nine and two shared aircraft
destroyed.

Beurling quickly latched onto a formation of four Macchis flying line astern, and promptly shot
down the rearmost fighter with a deflection shot. Its pilot was three-victory veteran Sergente
Maggiore Faliero Gelli of 378a Squadriglia, who survived by crash-landing his Macchi into a rocky
field on Gozo. He was found unconscious in the cockpit of his fighter by Gozitan locals who,
unusually, did not beat the pilot up or lynch him.

Gelli is believed to have been the only man to survive being shot down by Beurling. The Canadian
ace immediately destroyed another Macchi, whose pilot did not enjoy the same luck as Gelli. The final
moments of this particular action have been depicted in this specially commissioned artwork by Mark
Postlethwaite. Seven-victory ace Capitano Furio Niclot Doglio, commander of 151a Squadriglia, was
downed in spectacular fashion, as Beurling later noted in his Combat Report – 'the poor devil simply
blew to pieces in the air'.

Beurling was closing in on the next Macchi in the formation when he spotted two Bf 109Fs below
him. He immediately half-rolled and pulled up beneath them. In his words, 'I let the first guy have it
full-out and caught him in the gas tank. Down he went. I still had time for a shot at his teammate, and
blew pieces off his wings and tail. He flew off in a hurry, skidding all over the sky. What happened to
him God knows.'

Since Takali airfield was now covered in bomb craters, Beurling's squadron landed at nearby Luqa.
After quickly re-arming and refuelling, the Spitfires took off again, this time to meet a party of 20 Bf
109Fs. Beurling went after a separated rotte and destroyed one, with the second German fighter
credited to him as a probable. Two days later the Canadian ace destroyed yet another Bf 109F. Thus,
after nearly two months on the island, his score now stood at 16 destroyed, one probably destroyed
and four damaged, surpassing the score of Malta's previous 'ace of aces', Malayan-born Flt Sgt
'Paddy' Schade of No 126 Sqn.

CONTENTS

PROLOGUE

For 29 months during the darkest days of World War 2, the Mediterranean island of Malta endured an unrelenting siege. Cut-off, and almost written off, Malta endured and survived despite all odds. In the history of aerial warfare there has probably never been a closer link between a civilian population and its air defences.

This account focuses on the part played by Spitfire pilots and squadrons in the desperate defence of Malta in 1942. In a repeat of the Battle of the Britain two years earlier, the iconic Vickers-Supermarine fighter once again proved to be the deciding factor in the struggle for air supremacy over a strategically vital island. And as in the Battle of Britain, Malta was defended by literally a handful of fighter units that were opposed by a numerically superior enemy force that threatened invasion at almost any time.

Unlike in the Battle of Britain, however, the odds greatly favoured the German and Italian units, the fight lasted much longer and the RAF pilots involved endured greater stress and physical hardship when out of the cockpit. Indeed, veteran RAF ace Stan Turner, who was Wing Commander Flying at Takali in 1942, summed up his Malta experience in just four words – 'It was a bastard.'

The island of Malta had been the centrepiece of Britain's strategic naval plan for the Mediterranean for almost a century-and-a-half prior to the

This spectacular aerial view of Malta shows Grand Harbour and Valetta in the foreground and Marsaxlokk Bay in the distance. Hal Far airfield was to the right of Marsaxlokk Bay, and in this photograph it is marked out by the solitary white cloud directly above it (*via Frederick Galea and Brian Cull*)

commencement of World War 2. It possessed a first rate deep-water port in the form of Grand Harbour that provided a staging post for vessels heading to British territories in the Middle East and beyond.

However, with the development of air power between the wars, and the rise of fascism in nearby Italy, Malta appeared to be exposed and indefensible in the build up to World War 2. Indeed, much of the British government, and especially the Air Ministry, were ready to write it off. The only dissenting voice came from the Admiralty, which planned to upgrade the island's defences. Thus, the Committee for Imperial Defence put into motion a plan that would improve Malta's ability to fend off attack from the air. Central to this was the basing of four RAF fighter squadrons on the island, as well as the installation of 172 anti-aircraft guns. Work was also started on an all-weather airstrip at Luqa. Budgetary constraints quickly curtailed the committee's plans.

On 3 September 1939, when Great Britain declared war on Germany following the latter country's invasion of Poland, Malta's defences consisted of just seven submarines, 12 motor torpedo boats and a few minesweepers. There were no RAF fighters on the island. The power of the Italian *Regia Aeronautica* cast its shadow over Malta from the north, thus convincing the Admiralty that the island was too vulnerable to act as home for the Royal Navy's Mediterranean Fleet. It was decided that it would have to operate from Alexandria, in Egypt, leaving the western Mediterranean to the French Navy. However, in June 1940 France signed an armistice with Germany, and the British government hastily had to fill the vacuum left by the removal of the French fleet from the area by instructing Force 'H' to sortie into the Mediterranean from its base in Gibraltar.

The need for fighters to defend Malta had been expounded by Adm Sir Andrew Cunningham, Commander-in-Chief Mediterranean Fleet, and the island would duly come to depend on Adm Sir James Sommerville's Force 'H' for its protection. Despite the facilities provided by the Royal Navy, and the partial construction of two intersecting all-weather airstrips at Luqa, in addition to airfields at Takali and Hal Far, the RAF remained reluctant to base its fighter squadrons outside the United Kingdom.

In April 1940, Air Officer Commanding (AOC) on Malta, Air Cde F H M Maynard, received permission to use four crated Sea Gladiators that had been offloaded on the island from the aircraft carrier HMS *Glorious* earlier in the year. These machines subsequently formed the basis of the Hal Far Fighter Flight. Offensive capability at this time was provided by Fairey Swordfish of the recently formed 830 Naval Air Squadron.

On 11 June 1940, less than seven hours after Italy had declared war on the British Commonwealth, ten Savoia-Marchetti SM.79 bombers sortied against Grand Harbour and Hal Far air station. The Hal Far Fighter Flight's Sea Gladiators rose to intercept them, and so began a 29-month ordeal for the 250,000 citizens of Malta, and the Allied servicemen who defended them.

In reality, the *Regia Aeronautica* proved not to be as powerful as it had seemed pre-war, and the Italian Navy was also unable to prevent the movement of Allied convoys in the Mediterranean. Consequently, a small number of British fighters – initially a handful of Sea Gladiators

Air Cde F H M Maynard was the RAF's AOC Malta in 1940–41. Born and raised in New Zealand, he had seen action in World War 1 as an engineer in the Royal Naval Division, prior to being commissioned as a flight sub-lieutenant in the Royal Naval Air Service. A career officer, Maynard had risen to the rank of air vice-marshal by the time he retired from the RAF in late 1945 (*via Frederick Galea and Brian Cull*)

Hurricane I P3731/J was one of 12 Hawker fighters flown to Malta from the aircraft carrier HMS *Argus* as part of Operation *Hurry* on 2 August 1940. It was subsequently flown on a regular basis by Malta ace Sgt Fred Robertson – he claimed his sixth victory in it on 19 January 1941. At least two other aces made claims in the aircraft as well. Eventually passed on to newly formed No127 Sqn at Habbaniyah, in Iraq, in June 1941, P3731 was shot down by a Vichy French Dewoitine D.520 over Deir-es-Zor (on the banks of the Euphrates River) on 3 July (*via R C B Ashworth*)

taken over by the RAF, and then Hurricanes, which arrived on 21 June 1940 – were able to limit the air attacks on Malta itself, as well as on Allied shipping in local waters.

More Hurricanes had been received by August, and the Fighter Flight became No 261 Sqn. Although the Chiefs of Staff recognised that Malta would play a crucial role as an unsinkable base for aircraft tasked with tracking the movement of the Italian Fleet and disrupting Axis supply lines to North Africa, the reinforcement of the island's defences continued at a slow pace.

During this period, *Regia Aeronautica* raids against Grand Harbour and the surrounding airfields were desultory, and they failed to stop British convoys supplying Malta in the autumn of 1940. Air elements on the island now included Wellingtons, Marylands, Sunderlands and Swordfish, although the air defence still consisted of just No 261 Sqn and its 15 Hurricanes.

In November, the Marylands played a key role in reconnoitring the Italian Battle Fleet at Taranto before the Fleet Air Arm's famous strike on the night of the 11th. Despite this success, the overall combined air and sea offensive in the Mediterranean destroyed only 2.3 per cent of Italian supplies being sent to North Africa.

The British had reason for optimism for Malta's survival at year-end. This was to change, however, in early 1941 with the arrival of German forces in the Mediterranean.

'Faith, 'Hope' and 'Charity' – undoubtedly the most famous of all Gladiators, even if the legend is more myth than fact. These three Sea Gladiators of the Hal Far Fighter Flight, photographed here in June 1940, are N5520 (which survives to this day), N5531 and N5519 (*via J Pickering*)

FIRST *BLITZ*

When Hitler's attempt to defeat Great Britain had been foiled by the RAF in the summer and autumn of 1940, the Führer turned his attentions east. He now focused on preparations for the surprise invasion of the Soviet Union, planned for June 1941. However, his dissatisfaction with Italy's handling of the war in North Africa, Greece and the Mediterranean saw him to commit German forces to secure the southern flank well before the Wehrmacht invaded Russia.

The first unit sent south in late December 1940 was X *Fliegerkorps*, commanded by *General der Flieger* Hans Geisler. Transferred to Sicily, its primary mission was to deal with the British forces defending Malta.

The badly damaged HMS *Illustrious* (visible to the right of the dockyard crane) comes under sustained attack in Grand Harbor during the *'Illustrious Blitz'* of late January 1941. The Luftwaffe generated up to 80 sorties a day for ten straight days as X *Fliegerkorps* tried in vain to destroy the Royal Navy's newest aircraft carrier (*via Tim Addis*)

X *Fliegerkorps* controlled 80 Ju 88A-4 and 50 He 111H-6 bombers, 80 Ju 87R-1 dive-bombers and an undisclosed number of Bf 110C-4s assigned to III./ZG 26 at Palermo that were to act as fighter escorts for the bombers. In addition to the Luftwaffe assets on Sicily, the *Regia Aeronautica* committed 45 SM.79 bombers and 75 CR.42 and C.200 fighters to the order of battle.

X *Fliegerkorps* initially made its presence felt attacking a convoy of four supply vessels that left Gibraltar on 6 January 1941 as part of Operation *Excess*. These ships were escorted by Force 'H', which included the aircraft carrier HMS *Illustrious*. Three days out of port, while off the Algerian coast, *Illustrious* was hit by six 1100-lb bombs dropped from Ju 87s. Later that day it limped into Malta's Grand Harbour.

The ten days during which the badly damaged carrier took refuge in Grand Harbour became known as the *'Illustrious Blitz'*. The RAF and Fleet Air Arm were never able to put up more than six Hurricanes, a Sea Gladiator and four Fulmars to fend off the attacks by Axis bombers. The Luftwaffe generated up to 80 sorties per day against Malta during this period, with the *Regia Aeronautica* also making a significant effort to sink *Illustrious*. Somehow the carrier survived this onslaught, although its near loss graphically pointed out the need for an effective fighter force on the island to defend Allied shipping moored in Grand Harbour.

With Axis forces now clearly controlling the skies of the central Mediterranean, supply convoys to Malta were halted indefinitely and RAF efforts to use the island as a base from which to disrupt enemy supply lines had to be abandoned.

X *Fliegerkorps* continued its offensive against Grand Harbour and the airfields at Luqa, Takali and Hal Far into February. On the 9th of that month, 7./JG 26 and 1./JG 27, both equipped with Bf 109E-7s, began operating from Sicily as part of the planned final phase in the subjugation of Malta's defences.

Elsewhere in the Mediterranean, British forces were suffering a series of reversals at the hands of the Germans, who were proving to be a far more formidable enemy than the Italians had been. Field Marshal Sir Archibald Wavell's advance into Cyrenaica was halted in February by General Erwin Rommel's newly arrived *Afrika Korps*, which then launched a counteroffensive that drove British troops back into Egypt and started the first siege of Tobruk. In the Balkans, German forces invaded Yugoslavia and Greece, then landed on Crete.

With Axis domination of the eastern Mediterranean complete, X *Fliegerkorps* was transferred from Sicily to bases in Greece, Crete and Rhodes. This ultimately proved to be a major mistake on the part of the Luftwaffe, as it gave the embattled defenders of Malta a temporary stay of execution.

Prior to heading east, the German bombers had driven the Wellingtons off the island in March, while the Bf 109Es had neutralised

A bombing raid in progress in 1941. By the spring of 1942, Malta had earned the title of 'most bombed place on earth'. Spitfires for the air defence squadrons were seen as the only effective defence against raids such as this one. Fifteen Spitfires sent to Malta on 7 March 1942 would be the first of their type to see service outside the UK (*via Frederick Galea and Brian Cull*)

Pilots from No 261 Sqn kill time between sorties attempting to fix the tyres (possibly from the requisitioned Malta bus in the background) at Takali in the spring of 1941. The pilot standing at the extreme left of this group is Sgt Fred Robertson, who was the highest-scoring Hurricane ace of the Malta campaign, with ten victories (*via J Pickering*)

Hurricane IIB Z2961 of No 185 Sqn was yet another aircraft flown by several notable pilots over Malta, including Plt Off David Barnwell (five and two shared victories), Sgt Tony Boyd (five and two shared victories) and Sgt Gareth Horricks (seven and two shared victories) (*via P H P Roberts*)

the handful of No 261 Sqn Hurricanes that had remained airworthy despite a shortage of spare parts, fuel, ammunition and pilots. However, by the end of the month, with the bombing offensive having petered out, the situation on Malta for the RAF had started to improve. On the 23rd a supply convoy had made it through from Gibraltar, and in April 35 Hurricane IIAs flew off the deck of the aircraft carrier HMS *Ark Royal* into Malta. With the Luftwaffe's attention diverted elsewhere, Wellingtons, Blenheims and Beauforts began to fly anti-shipping strikes from the island again, and the Royal Navy also sent four destroyers to operate from Malta.

AVM H P Lloyd arrived to take over from AVM Maynard in May, and a new phase in Malta's defence began. A total of 47 Hurricanes were flown in that month, allowing No 261 Sqn and No 1430 Flight to combine as No 185 Sqn at Hal Far. The unit was in turn joined by No 249 Sqn, which was led out from the UK by Sqn Ldr R A Barton.

By the early summer of 1941, Malta had once again became a base from which Axis supply lines to North Africa could be interdicted by Allied air, submarine and surface forces.

MALTA ON THE OFFENSIVE

In June, *Luftflotte* 4 departed for the Russian front, by which point X *Fleigerkorps* had shifted to the eastern Mediterranean. The offensive against Malta was once again left to the *Regia Aeronautica*. Despite the now reduced threat of invasion, the RAF continued to send more Hurricane IIs to bolster units on the island – 43 arrived in early June, followed by more at the end of the month. Still more fighters allowed

No 126 Sqn to be formed at Takali, and offensive operations were stepped up with Wellingtons conducting night bombing raids and Swordfish flying anti-shipping strikes. Blenheims were also sent out to Malta from the UK to perform anti-shipping strikes, and although these missions proved to be highly successful, they were also costly in terms of aircraft and aircrew lost.

Two convoys arrived in July and September, bringing supplies – but no food or fuel – to sustain Malta through to March 1942.

The offensive forces based on the island were now inflicting mounting losses on Axis supply convoys sailing between Italy and North Africa. In March 1941, the enemy was losing about 10 per cent of its tonnage in the Mediterranean to Malta-based ships, submarines and aircraft, but this figure rose to 270,000 tons between June and September. Things got worse in October and November, when 127,000 tons per month (20 per cent of all materials sent from Italy to Axis forces in North Africa) was lost.

In the autumn of 1941, British forces were planning for a new offensive just as Rommel's army prepared to eliminate Tobruk and drive on to the Suez Canal. The Italian High Command had been infuriated by the premature transfer of X *Fliegerkorps* to the eastern Mediterranean in the spring of that year, and now Rommel was pressing for additional air power to ensure the neutralisation of Malta once and for all. As if to reinforce his point, he complained to the Wehrmacht HQ in Berlin that the continued decimation of his supply lines would prevent the possibility of any further German offensives in North Africa.

Two factors led to a rethinking of the Luftwaffe's aerial strategy in the Mediterranean, which had initially been shaped by the prospect of the campaign in North Africa being both short and successful. First, the now apparent lack of progress in the theatre was due to the tenuousness of Axis supply lines, which were vulnerable to interference by Malta-based aircraft. The new Allied *Crusader* offensive, launched in November 1941, had relieved Tobruk and sent Axis forces into retreat. Following closely on the heels of this defeat was the foundering of the German push on Moscow just weeks later.

Second, compounding these twin disasters was the entry of the United States into the war on the side of the Allies following Japan's surprise attack on Pearl Harbor on 7 December 1941. Senior military planners in Germany now realised that a long war stretched ahead of them. And to allow the Axis war machine to function throughout the years of conflict that potentially lay ahead, a reliable source of oil was required. Beyond Suez lay the oil fields of the Middle East. It was hoped that an all-out offensive in southern Russia, launched in conjunction with a new North African campaign, would secure this oil for the Third Reich. A preliminary objective of any new offensive by Rommel would be the elimination of Malta.

In December 1941, *Luftflotte* 2, under the command of General Feldmarschall Albert Kesselring, was transferred from the central Russian front to Sicily in preparation for a new offensive against Malta. Subordinate to *Luftflotte* 2 were Sicily-based II *Fliegerkorps*, led by General Major Bruno Loerzer, and X *Fliegerkorps*, still operating in the eastern Mediterranean. These units were brought up to a combined strength of 650 aircraft, 400 of which were based on Sicily.

SPITFIRES INTO THE BREACH

RAF assets on Malta in January 1942 comprised Nos 126 and 249 Sqns at Takali and No 185 Sqn at Hal Far, all of which were equipped with Hurricanes, Nos 40 and 104 Sqns with Wellington IIs at Luqa and the Marylands of No 69 Sqn, also at Luqa. Radar coverage of the approaches to Malta was now provided by three Air Ministry Experimental Stations at Dingli, Maddealena and Ta Silch, with two more added in February on nearby Fanuma and Gozo.

Pitted against this force was II *Fliegerkorps*, with its 120 Bf 109F-4s assigned to JG 53 and 40 Bf 109F-4s of II./JG 3. II *Fliegerkorps'* bombing element consisted of *Stab* I./KG 54, *Stab*, II. and III./KG 77 and KGr 606 and 806 with 200 Ju 88A-4s. And from February 1942, III./StG 3 and its 40 Ju 87D-1s were operational in North Africa.

The battle plan of II *Fliegerkorps* was similar to that devised for *Luftflotten* 2 and 3 at the beginning of the Battle of Britain. First, it was to achieve air supremacy through the elimination of Malta's fighter squadrons. Second, it would throw the full weight of the bomber force against the harbour installations, communications and radar sites, stores depots and other military objectives. Last, it would provide aerial cover for the paratroop drop and amphibious invasion, codenamed Operation *Hercules*, planned for May 1942.

The Luftwaffe's offensive began in mid-January 1942, although at first it was limited by bad weather. An average of just 65 sorties per day was achieved by the 40 Ju 88s initially involved in the campaign, although they attacked their objectives without any significant harassment by RAF fighters due to the effective standing patrols that were being flown over Malta by Sicily-based Bf 109s. And these aircraft also inflicted a heavy toll on the Wellington and Blenheim squadrons operating in the area to the point where, in March, they were declared non-operational.

The Hurricane IIs equipping the three fighter squadrons on Malta were both outclassed and outnumbered three-to-one by the Bf 109F-4s. Indeed, the only thing that saved the Hurricanes from total annihilation was poor weather. Eighty squadrons of Spitfires were available in the UK, but none had yet been sent overseas. Malta was

Some of Malta's earliest, and most notable, Spitfire pilots. They are, from left to right, Channel Islander Flg Off Raoul Daddo-Langlois, Canadian Flg Off Norman Lee, Australian Sgt Paul Brennan, New Zealander Sgt Ray Hesselyn and Englishman Flt Lt Laddie Lucas (*via Patrick Lee*)

AVM H P Lloyd was AOC Malta from June 1941 through to July of the following year. Like his predecessor Air Cde F H M Maynard, Lloyd had seen action in World War 1 as a sapper, although he had served with the Royal Engineers. Commissioned in the Royal Flying Corps in 1917, Lloyd had received the MC and DFC by war's end. Seeing much service in India during the interwar period, Lloyd also held various senior posts during World War 2. AOC Bomber Command in his final year in the RAF, Lloyd retired with the rank of Air Chief Marshal in 1950 (*via Frederick Galea*)

The advent of streamlined slipper tanks at last allowed short-ranged Spitfire Vs to be ferried from aircraft carriers to Malta in early 1942. This particular fighter (BR202) is fitted with a 170-gallon tank, and is seen here undertaking a test flight from Boscombe Down (*via B Robertson*)

considered a backwater by the RAF in early 1942, but it soon became obvious that only the replacement of obsolete Hurricane IIs with Spitfire Vs would allow the fighter units on Malta to defend the island from aerial attack.

The arrival in Malta of a No 10 Sqn RAAF Sunderland from Gibraltar on 16 February was key in setting the stage for both the eventual delivery of Spitfires and the upgrading of the aerial tactics employed by the defending fighter squadrons to the standard of UK-based units. Amongst the passengers aboard the flying boat were seven pilots who would go on to enjoy great success in Spitfires over Malta. These men were Flt Lt P B 'Laddie' Lucas, Flg Off Raoul 'Daddy-Longlegs' Daddo-Langlois, Canadian Plt Off R W 'Buck' McNair, Rhodesian Flg Off G A F 'Buck' Buchanan, Australian Sgt A P 'Tim' Goldsmith, New Zealander Plt Off J G 'Ronnie' West and, most importantly, Sqn Ldr Stanley 'Bull' Turner.

Turner, a 28-year-old Canadian, had seen action flying Hurricanes with No 242 Sqn over Dunkirk and during the Battle of Britain under the dynamic leadership of Sqn Ldr Douglas Bader. Later, he led Spitfire-equipped No 145 Sqn on 'Circus' operations in 1941. AOC Malta, AVM H P Lloyd, had requested that a highly experienced fighter leader be sent to Malta, and Turner filled the bill. He took over No 249 Sqn at Takali, and immediately imparted his knowledge of RAF Fighter Command's latest tactics and procedures to his pilots.

Gone was the inefficient line astern three-aeroplane section, replaced by the line abreast four-fighter section comprised of two leader/wingman elements. Pilots would now also form up south of the island so as to be up sun when they carried out their interceptions. Head-on attacks against bombers were taught too, as this had proven to be the most effective way of breaking up an enemy formation. Turner's dynamic and inspiring leadership was one of the turning points in the siege of Malta.

AVM Lloyd's repeated demands for Spitfires were finally heeded at around the time Turner and his fellow arrivals were selected for transfer to Malta. Some 16 Vickers-Supermarine fighters were packed into crates and despatched to Gibraltar in the hold of the merchantman *Cape Hawke*, accompanied by 18 pilots and many more groundcrew. This group was led by Battle of Britain veteran, and future ace, Sqn Ldr Stan Grant, and the vessel arrived at Gibraltar on 22 February. The new Spitfire Mk VBs, tropicalised with Vokes air filters for desert conditions, underwent final assembly aboard the aircraft carrier HMS *Eagle*. Once rebuilt, each of the fighters was fitted with a 90-gallon slipper tank beneath its fuselage – these were the first such tanks to be used in the frontline.

Like the reinforcement flights of Hurricanes sent to Malta the previous year, the Spitfires were going to be launched 700 miles from the beleaguered island so as to ensure that *Eagle* stayed out of range of Axis bombers. Flt Lt Norman MacQueen and Flg Off Norman

Right and below
Spitfire VBs take off from HMS *Eagle* on the second of the delivery runs to Malta, code-named Operation *Picket I*, on 21 March 1942. Only nine fighters were delivered on this date (*via B Robertson*)

The pilots of Operation *Picket I* head for their Spitfires tied down on the stern of HMS *Eagle* prior to departing for Malta on 21 March 1942. Sixteen fighters were meant to be sent, but the Blenheim escort for the second flight failed to find the carrier due to poor weather. The pilot in the foreground wearing a 'Mae West' adorned with the head of a panda is Sgt John 'Slim' Yarra. Second from the right is Sqn Ldr E J 'Jumbo' Gracie and on the extreme right is Flt Lt Tim Johnston. Gracie was a gruff, no-nonsense character who was a mainstay in the early months of the siege. Arriving with *Picket I*, he took over command of No 126 Sqn. He was instrumental in overseeing the safe arrival of a large reinforcement of Spitfires to the island from USS *Wasp*, and also for demanding that the Spitfires be painted in a more suitable overall blue/grey camouflage scheme, instead of their remaining in desert colours. Gracie later commanded the Takali Wing, and was a very popular and inspiring leader. He failed to return from a mission to Germany on 15 February 1944 whilst at the controls of a No 169 Sqn Mosquito. In the background can be seen Spitfire VB AB340 (*IWM*)

Lee had been flown to Gibraltar from Malta to help lead in the Spitfires, so the least experienced pilots in Grant's group (Sgts M Irving Gass and H J Fox) were left behind.

On the night of 26 February *Eagle* set sail, escorted by Force 'H', which consisted of the battleship HMS *Malaya*, the cruiser HMS *Hermione*, nine destroyers and the elderly training carrier HMS *Argus*. The following day, as preparations were made to launch the Spitfires, it was discovered that the 90-gallon tanks were malfunctioning – the fuel was being siphoned off into the air stream instead of into the engine. The force returned to Gibraltar, and a specialist was rushed out to rectify the problem. The whole thing was attempted again on 7 March (code-named Operation *Spotter*).

A single Spitfire (AB333) went unserviceable when it came time to launch the aircraft, and it was left behind with its pilot, Australian (and future ace) Sgt Jack 'Slim' Yarra. The remaining 15 fighters, split into three flights of five aircraft, arrived at Takali unscathed. They were led in by Sqn Ldr Stan Grant and his two flight commanders, Norman

MacQueen and Philip 'Nip' Heppell. Amongst the remaining pilots were Australian Sgt Paul Brennan, his friend New Zealander Sgt Ray Hesselyn, Greek-Rhodesian Plt Off Ioannis Agorastos 'Johnny' Plagis and Englishman Plt Off Peter Nash. All of these men would become aces in the coming weeks, but not all of them would survive through to June. A new phase in the fight for Malta was about to begin.

THE THIN BLUE LINE

As the newly arrived pilots tried to familiarise themselves with their surroundings, their Spitfires were stripped of their long-range tanks, serviced for combat (including having their guns harmonised) and repainted in a colour scheme better suited to maritime operations. The paint used for this task has been described as grey-blue in colour. Once repainted, each aircraft had No 249 Sqn's 'GN' two-letter code applied to its fuselage sides.

It soon dawned on the Spitfire pilots that they were in a very different theatre from the one they had just left in southern England. Maltese children followed them everywhere, making buzzing sounds to emulate Spitfires. Big things were expected of the new aircraft, and those flying them, in the coming days, and there would be no shortage of targets.

First combat for the Spitfires came on 10 March at 1020 hrs. Nine Ju 88s had entered Malta's airspace with a Bf 109 escort, and three of the bombers targeted Luqa and destroyed the last Wellington remaining on the island. Seven Spitfires – three led by Sqn Ldr Turner and four by Flt Lt 'Nip' Heppell – were scrambled, along with eight Hurricanes of No 126 Sqn and four from No 185 Sqn. The Spitfires quickly climbed to 19,000 ft and Heppell's section soon spotted the Ju 88s, with their Bf 109 escort, below them.

The No 249 Sqn pilots duly bounced the enemy fighters from II. and III./JG 53, Heppell (in AB262/GN-B) firing a long burst and downing an aircraft from 8./JG 53. Plt Offs Peter Nash (in AB335/GN-F) and 'Johnny' Plagis (in AB346/GN-K) both claimed fighters as probables,

Spitfire VB AB264 was one of the first 15 Vickers-Supermarine fighters flown into Malta from HMS *Eagle* on 7 March 1942. Like most other Spitfires produced at this time that were destined for service in North Africa, this aircraft left the factory in the standard desert colour scheme of Middle Stone and Dark Earth, but with Sky Blue undersides instead of the more common Azure Blue. Sky Blue was best described as a light powder blue, and not at all like standard Sky. Indeed, it was similar to Luftwaffe RLM 76. On landing in Malta, the March delivery Spitfires were said to have been repainted in 'dark grey' (presumably Extra Dark Sea Grey), with white codes and serial numbers, but with the Sky Blue undersides left untouched. Plt Off Peter Nash destroyed a Ju 87 on 25 March in AB264 for his first confirmed kill on Malta, and Flt Lt 'Buck' McNair used the fighter to claim a share in the destruction of a Ju 88 the very next day (*via Frederick Galea*)

while Flg Off Daddo-Langlois (in GN-D) claimed one damaged. Peter Nash, who had been on the staff of *The Times* newspaper pre-war when aged just 18, recorded in his diary;

'I was No 2 to Heppell, with Plagis and Leggo (Rhodesian Plt Off Doug Leggo) three and four. We scrambled at about 1020 hrs, got up to 21,000 ft and saw three Ju 88s and some '109s about 4000 ft below us. A lovely bounce. Heppell got one and Plagis and I got a probable each, but Leggo missed his. I think we shook them up quite a bit. Plagis did well to knock one off my tail!'

A veteran of previous frontline tours with Nos 65 and 609 Sqns in 1941, Nash had received orders to No 249 Sqn in January 1942. With his tally already standing at two victories, one probable and three damaged by the time he arrived in Malta, he would quickly become one of the first pilots to achieve 'acedom' on the island.

Attempts to intercept two subsequent raids by German aircraft on 10 March were unsuccessful, even though the Hal Far Officers' Mess and Quarters was hit during the second attack. The fourth raid of the day, which arrived over Malta at 1632 hrs, was engaged, however. Forty Ju 88s, with Bf 109 escorts, hit Luqa and Hal Far, and they were set upon by four Spitfires and 11 Hurricanes. Flt Lt MacQueen and Flg Off Buchanan (in AB262 GN-B) each damaged Ju 88s, but AB343/GN-D, flown by Australian Plt Off Ken Murray, was shot down by either Hauptmann Karl-Heinz Krahl, *Gruppenkommandeur* of II./JG 3, or Feldwebel Hans Schade of 8./JG 53 (both German pilots were aces).

The canopy of Murray's parachute was partially collapsed by the slipstream of a Bf 109 that passed close by him, and he died in hospital of his injuries that evening. Twenty-year-old RAAF pilot Ken Murray of Toorak, Victoria, had become the first Spitfire pilot to die in the defence of Malta. 'Buck' Buchanan's Spitfire was also shot up by Bf 109s and its pilot wounded in the right leg, but not severely, whilst protecting the air-sea rescue launch that was sent out to pick up Murray – the latter had in fact come down on dry land.

At the end of the Spitfire's first operational day on Malta, No 249 Sqn's scoreboard stood at one enemy aircraft confirmed destroyed for the loss of one aircraft and its pilot.

More action on 11 March resulted in Sqn Ldr Grant being credited with a probable Bf 109 kill whilst flying AB262/GN-B and Sgt Hesselyn (in AB346/GN-K) damaging a second Messerschmitt

Plt Off Peter Nash of No 249 Sqn had been on the staff of *The Times* pre-war. Volunteering for the RAF in 1940, he destroyed Bf 109s on 13 October and 7 November 1941 with No 609 Sqn, prior to leaving for Malta in the new year – Nash piloted one of the first 15 Spitfires to reach the island. He was also one of the first Spitfire pilots to claim five confirmed victories on Malta. Nash duly downed four and one shared Bf 109s, four Ju 87s and one Ju 88 in two months of combat. Having participated in the crucial air battles of 9 and 10 May, Nash downed his final aircraft (a Bf 109) on 17 May, but was subsequently shot down and killed later that same day (*via Frederick Galea*)

Flg Off George Buchanan, seen here sat in the cockpit of Spitfire VB AB451/GN-T, had been a policeman in Rhodesia pre-war. Having served with No 41 Sqn in the UK, he arrived on Malta in February 1942. Posted to No 249 Sqn, Buchanan initially flew Hurricanes but did not start scoring until the unit switched to Spitfires. During March, April and May he claimed six destroyed, three probables and five damaged, in addition to a shared kill from his previous tour on the Channel front with No 41 Sqn (*RAF Museum*)

fighter. His aircraft was in turn hit by a single machine gun round behind the cockpit. One of the Spitfires was damaged on the ground at Takali the following day when three Ju 88s bombed the base. No claims were made by No 249 Sqn on 12 or 13 March.

A shuffle in command arrangements took place on the 14th when Takali Wing CO, Hurricane ace Wg Cdr A C 'Sandy' Rabagliati, reached the end of his tour and departed for the UK that evening. His place was taken by Sqn Ldr Turner, who handed over command of No 249 Sqn to Sqn Ldr Grant.

That morning, at 1030 hrs, three Ju 88s of II./KG 77, escorted by 20 Bf 109s, were detected by radar approaching the island. A further 15 German fighters were also picked up as they conducted a sea-search for two missing pilots that had been downed by flak, and a subsequent mid-air collision, while escorting a Ju 88 on a reconnaissance flight earlier that morning.

Four Spitfires were immediately scrambled to intercept the raid, although they actually engaged three of the sea-search Bf 109s over Gozo. Flt Lt MacQueen dived on one and fired off all of his ammunition in a single pass that saw him close to within 50 yards of the German fighter. He witnessed strikes along the Bf 109's fuselage, and Unteroffizier Adolf Jennerich, who was flying the 7./JG 53 machine, baled out. This success gave Norman MacQueen his first victory.

Having joined the RAF immediately upon the outbreak of war, MacQueen had served with Nos 610 and 602 Sqns (the latter as a flight commander) in 1940–41, before being posted to Malta. His solitary claim on the Channel front had been for a Bf 109F damaged over north-ern France in September 1941. MacQueen's previous combat experience quickly paid off, as he became one of the leading Spitfire aces over Malta in the spring of 1942. Both popular and well liked, he was an early mainstay of No 249 Sqn.

More Bf 109s were encountered during two patrols mounted during the afternoon of 14 March, with two being claimed as damaged by Flt Lt Lucas (flying GN-G).

NEW TACTICS

Following the arrival of Spitfires on Malta, senior fighter tacticians on the island had soon implemented a procedure that had prevailed during the Battle of Britain. When an enemy formation was detected, four Spitfires would be scrambled and told to climb to 20,000 ft. From this height they would have an advantage over the fighter escorts protecting the German bombers. Whilst they were providing high cover, whatever Hurricanes were available would be sent in at medium altitude to attack the Ju 88s.

Just such an interception occurred on the morning of 15 March, when three Ju 88s and their escorts targeted Luqa and Valetta. Four Spitfires, led by Flt Lts W C 'Bud' Connell (a Canadian pilot who had just transferred over to No 249 Sqn from No 126 Sqn), and seven Hurricanes engaged the aircraft in low cloud. A Bf 109 and Ju 88 were damaged. That afternoon, Connell (in AB346/GN-K) was again in the thick of the action when his four-aircraft formation attacked three Ju 88s and seven Bf 109s sent to bomb Zabbar. He claimed a bomber probably destroyed, and German records indicate that a Ju 88 from 3./KGr 806 failed to

Flt Lt Norman MacQueen had served with Nos 610 and 602 Sqns prior to being posted to Malta as part of Operation *Spotter* on 7 March 1942. He was one No 249 Sqn's most successful pilots in its early weeks of Spitfire operations from the island, scoring his first victory on 14 March (a Bf 109 over Gozo). Two more Messerschmitts followed later that month, and in April MacQueen destroyed three Ju 88s and one and one shared Bf 109s. Claiming another share in the destruction of a Bf 109 on 1 May, this victory took his tally to seven and two shared destroyed and four and four shared damaged. Throughout MacQueen's short career his aircraft had never been hit by enemy fire. However, his luck deserted him on 4 May, when his formation was bounced by Bf 109s from III./JG 53. One dived through the Spitfires and then pulled up and fired a quick snap shot into the underside of MacQueen's Spitfire (BR226). Briefly faltering, the No 249 Sqn ace managed to fly his aircraft almost all the way back to Takali before diving into the ground just short of the airfield. It was thought that MacQueen had been wounded in the attack and eventually lost consciousness. A popular, well-liked individual, his loss was a great blow to No 249 Sqn (*via Frederick Galea*)

return from this mission. Six Spitfires and eight Hurricanes engaged still more Ju 88s and Bf 109s in a late afternoon raid on the 15th, although no claims were made by No 249 Sqn pilots following a brief skirmish.

Revealing that 'Spitfire snobbery' was alive and well in the Mediterranean now that the Vickers-Supermarine fighter had made its combat debut in this theatre, pilots from JG 53 were credited with three such kills on 14 and 15 March, despite No 249 Sqn having lost no aircraft on either date.

Following no interceptions of the 16 raids launched by Ju 88s on Malta on the 16th, RAF fighter pilots enjoyed better fortune on 17 March. The highlight for No 249 Sqn was the destruction of a Bf 109 by future ace Sgt Paul Brennan (flying AB346/GN-K), who later recalled;

'I started turning with them. One was in front, the other behind. Round and round we went. Suddenly, the one in front decided to go up-sun. Luckily for me, he was not quite certain where I was. As he straightened up, I was 100 ft below and 200 yards behind him, dead astern. As I pulled a bead on him, tracer from the other '109 whipped past my port wingtip. I could see my explosive cannon shells and machine gun bullets bursting along the front fuselage, behind the cockpit and on the port wing root of my target. I gave him six seconds – a long burst. For a moment or two the '109 seemed to hang, then it dived straight down.'

The Luftwaffe *Blitz* on Malta at this time was intense, with 15 separate raids being sent against the island on the 17th between 0733 hrs and 1842 hrs. This amounted to 54 Ju 88 sorties, and the bombers were escorted by standing patrols of Bf 109s, which were ordered to hunt down any Spitfires or Hurricanes audacious enough to venture into what had now effectively become German airspace.

Aside from Brennan's victory, Sqn Ldr Grant and Plt Off Plagis (in AB335/GN-F) claimed two Bf 109s damaged during a later raid on 17 March. However, these successes came at a price, as Scotsman Flt Sgt Ian Cormack was lost that same day when AB330/GN-C failed to pull out of a dive and crashed into the sea off Filfla.

More action was to follow on the 18th, and in a series of fighter-versus-fighter clashes, Flt Lt MacQueen was credited with the destruction of a Bf 109F from *Stab* III./JG 53. The pilot of this aircraft, Leutnant Kurt Lauinger, had just shot down 20-year-old Liverpudlian Plt Off Harry Fox (in AB334/GN-J), who baled out into the sea and was lost – the wounded Lauinger was rescued, however. Two Bf 109s and a Ju 88 were also damaged by pilots from No 249 Sqn.

Three Spitfires had been lost and two damaged on the ground during bombing raids in the ten days since the 15 aircraft had entered combat. Only a handful now remained serviceable.

On 20 March the Luftwaffe launched a four-day *Blitz* against key Maltese airfields, which the Germans hoped would eradicate recent improvements made by the Allies as they attempted to strengthen the aerial defences of the embattled island. It would be a day of triumph and tragedy for No 249 Sqn in particular.

Rhodesian pilot Plt Off Doug Leggo showed up at the airfield early that morning, having spent the night drinking and in the company of a female friend. Despite having had no sleep in 24 hours, he was scheduled to be on readiness. Fellow Rhodesian 'Johnny' Plagis tried to persuade him not to fly, but Leggo would have none of it.

Canadian Plt Off Robert 'Buck' McNair served with No 411 Sqn from June 1941 through to February 1942, when he was sent to Malta in a Sunderland flying boat. Upon the arrival of the first Spitfires on the island, he was posted to No 249 Sqn. McNair quickly ran up a score of seven victories (to add to his previous kill with No 411 Sqn) prior to being posted back to his old unit in the UK in mid-June. He scored eight more victories with the 2nd Tactical Air Force's No 421 Sqn in 1943, prior to spending the rest of the war as a staff officer in RCAF Overseas HQ (*via Frederick Galea*)

At 0805 hrs, four Spitfires (one of which was flown by Leggo) and 12 Hurricanes took off to intercept Bf 109s. Future ace Plt Off 'Buck' McNair (in AB341/GN-E) quickly spotted a lone Messerschmitt and promptly shot down Unteroffizier Josef Fankhauser of 7./JG 53 as he attempted to turn away from the RAF fighters – the German aircraft crashed into the sea off Delimara. The Canadian's combat report for his first Malta victory read as follows:

'The '109 went into a spiral dive, and looking around and seeing no other Huns about, I went down after it, having no trouble in following. I waited my chance to fire again, and got a good burst into it. I saw hits on the starboard wing, and pieces came off, but he still didn't take any evasive action – he just continued with the spiral dive down to 3000 ft. I started clobbering the '109 all over. I emptied my cannon and continued with the machine guns. Oil and glycol from its cooling system poured out. The white glycol looked beautiful streaming out into the clear air – it was a really lovely day.'

In contrast to McNair, who was clearly enjoying himself, Doug Leggo was having trouble keeping up with his squadronmates. He was quickly singled out by another German *Jagdflieger*, who dived on the lone Spitfire (AB337) out of the sun and opened fire at a range of just 50 yards. The Spitfire was mortally damaged, and Leggo took to his parachute. However, another Bf 109 swooped down and either fired at the Rhodesian or collapsed the canopy of his parachute with his slipstream and Leggo plunged to his death.

Rhodesian Flg Off George Buchanan was joined by his compatriots Sgt Ioannis 'Johnny' Plagis and Plt Off Doug Leggo on 7 March 1942 when the latter two participated in Operation *Spotter*. Although Plagis had been raised in Rhodesia by Greek parents, and wore a Rhodesian flash on his uniform, he did not become a Rhodesian citizen until after the war. Doug Leggo would be killed in combat on 20 March in circumstances for which his close friend 'Johnny' Plagis felt responsible (*via Frederick Galea*)

'Johnny' Plagis was distraught, and blamed himself for the death of his friend. Indeed, he vowed to 'shoot down ten for Doug – I will too, if it takes me a lifetime.' It was also said that a Canadian pilot later strafed a German bomber crew in their life raft in retaliation for Leggo's death.

The pressure on the airfields continued on the morning of the 21st, with 106 Ju 88s, escorted by a similar number of Bf 109s, attacking Takali between 0845 hrs and 1015 hrs. Eight B110s of III./ZG 26, protected by 35 Bf 109s, bombed and strafed Hal Far shortly after the last of the Ju 88s had departed. These attacks were flown on the heels of a large raid (63 Ju 88s) against Takali at 1830 hrs the previous evening.

The first carpet-bombing on Malta was obviously meant to impede the arrival of nine Spitfires flown off *Eagle* earlier that day in

an operation codenamed *Picket I* – 16 were meant to be sent, but the Blenheim escort for the second flight failed to find the carrier due to poor weather. Led by Hurricane ace Sqn Ldr E J 'Jumbo' Gracie, and including the previously bumped Sgt 'Slim' Yarra, the reinforcements arrived none too soon, as that morning yet another Spitfire had been damaged in the raid on Takali. No 249 Sqn was now down to just two serviceable aircraft.

Takali was hit again at 1435 hrs, when 70 Ju 88s targeted the airfield. Spitfire AB331 and four Hurricanes were destroyed and damage inflicted on five more No 249 Sqn fighters and 15 Hurricanes. In addition, five pilots were killed when a large bomb fell just outside the front door of the Point de Vue Hotel in Rabat, which had been requisitioned to billet RAF officers stationed at nearby Takali. Those killed outright included Flg Off John Booth and Plt Off Jimmy Guerin of No 249 Sqn and Flt Lt Cecil Baker and Plt Off Hollis Hallett of No 126 Sqn. Hurricane pilot Plt Off Eddie Streets succumbed to his wounds in hospital.

Narrowly escaping death were 'Buck' McNair, 'Bud' Connell and Ronnie West, who had just entered the hotel lobby from the road when the bomb hit. As McNair later recalled;

'The realisation of what had happened began to dawn very slowly. My left arm had gone out of joint when I was blown 20–30 ft upstairs by the bomb, but I shoved it back into place. "Ronnie" and I sat on the kerbside and talked about it. As we discussed it, we began to understand the awfulness of it all. Then we started cursing the bloody Huns – it was maddening to think that all we could do to them was curse. We were inwardly sick, sick at heart. We decided to get drunk. When we got over to the mess, the orderly refused us anything to drink and wouldn't open the bar. We broke our way in and each took a bottle of *White Horse* whiskey. We drank gulps of it straight, and it helped relieve the tension.'

In the aftermath of these raids, it was feared that Takali would be out of action for a week. However, troops worked through the night and into the next day to make the runway serviceable enough for the surviving airworthy Spitfires and Hurricanes to be flown out to Luqa – the aircraft departed for the latter base on the evening of 22 March.

The new fighters flown in from *Eagle* were intended to allow No 126 Sqn to copy No 249 Sqn and reform as a Spitfire unit. However, the high rate of attrition experienced by the latter squadron, combined with the reduced number of aircraft that reached Malta, meant that there simply were not enough Spitfires to go round. So, for the time being, Nos 249 and 126 Sqn would have to share the few serviceable Spitfires on the island. There was now a preponderance of Spitfire pilots and too few aircraft to go around, so a handful with Hurricane experience (including 'Slim' Yarra) temporarily joined No 185 Sqn, which was then short of aviators.

With Takali out of commission, and RAF fighter operations temporarily halted, Wg Cdr Turner took this opportunity to revise tactics yet again. As in the Battle of Britain, it had been common practice since the arrival of Spitfires on the island to send the less speedy Hurricanes after the bombers, while No 249 Sqn took on the Bf 109 escorts. However, the experience of the previous few days had shown that the Hurricane IIBs were too slow and lightly armed (the few Mk IICs on

Malta had had two of their four cannons removed to try and improve the fighter's performance) to take on the nimble Ju 88s.

So far, the heavily outnumbered Spitfires were trading kills at a one-to-one ratio with the Bf 109F escorts. Turner and Gracie, along with other senior pilots, reasoned that II *Fliegerkorps* would be harder hit if it lost more bombers than fighters, and Malta would be better off too. It was therefore decided that the wisest course of action was to send *all* Hurricanes and Spitfires straight for the bombers, avoiding the fighter escort wherever possible.

On 22–23 March, in a break from defending their airfields, Nos 126, 185 and 249 Sqns attempted to protect Convoy MW10, which had set out from the Egyptian port of Alexandria on 20 March with urgent supplies for Malta. Five Fleet Air Arm Albacore torpedo-bombers based on the island were sent out on the 22nd to attack Italian warships that were threatening the convoy. These vulnerable biplanes were escorted by three Spitfires, and shortly after take-off the formation was bounced by two Bf 109s. Flt Lt MacQueen quickly got onto the tail of one of the Messerschmitts and shot it down. Short on fuel following this engagement, the Spitfires broke off and returned home – two hours later the Albacores were recalled as well.

With the battered convoy nearing Malta on the morning of the 23rd, no fewer than 14 Spitfires and 11 Hurricanes were made ready to defend both the island and the vessels of MW10. Operating in pairs at 30-minute intervals over the ships, the fighter pilots reported contacts with 60 Ju 88s and 25 Bf 109s during the course of the day. Future ace Flt Lt 'Tim' Johnston, with Plt Off Mike Graves as his wingman, claimed No 126 Sqn's first Spitfire victory when, at 0910 hrs, he spotted a lone Ju 88 from reconnaissance unit 1(F)./122 and shot it down.

In the early afternoon, No 249 Sqn's Flt Lt MacQueen and Plt Off R H Sergeant joined two Hurricanes in attacking three Ju 88s. They were all damaged but managed to escape in cloud. Plt Off Plagis (in BP846) and Plt Off J E Peck of No 126 Sqn claimed another Junkers bomber damaged a short while later. 3./KG 54 reported the loss of one of its Ju 88s after it was set upon by four Spitfires, so one of these 'damaged' claims resulted in a victory. Johnston and Graves engaged three more Ju 88s during a mid-afternoon patrol on the 23rd, and the latter claimed the first of his four kills when he downed an aircraft from 3./KGr 806.

With much of the convoy in Malta's Grand Harbour by 24 May, the Luftwaffe sent Ju 88s, recently arrived Ju 87s and Bf 109 *Jabos* (fighter-bombers) to sink them at their moorings. Some 200+ sorties were flown by the enemy, and No 126 Sqn's Plt Offs Jimmy Peck and Don McLeod (both Americans) succeeded in downing two Bf 109F fighter-bombers from 10./JG 53 over Kalafrana Bay. Flg Off Buchanan of No 249 Sqn later damaged another Messerschmitt, but Sgt G S Bolton of No 126 Sqn was forced to crash-land after being shot up. Flt Lt Johnston also lodged a probable claim for a Ju 87D from III./StG 3.

Three Stukas and a Bf 109 were claimed destroyed by Grant (one of each), Plagis (a Ju 87) and Nash (also a Ju 87) of No 249 Sqn on 25 March, with No 126 Sqn's McLeod also getting a Messerschmitt fighter. Two more Ju 87s and two Ju 88s were destroyed the following day, with pilots from No 249 Sqn sharing in the destruction of three of

Australian Plt Off John Bisley of No 126 Sqn receives a DFC from the Governor of Malta, Field Marshal Lord Gort (Commander-in-Chief of all Allied forces on Malta) in June 1942. Bisley was credited with 5.5 victories over the island before returning to Australia in late 1942. He subsequently downed a Japanese G4M 'Betty' bomber off the coast of northern Australia while serving with No 452 Sqn on 20 June 1943 (*via Frederick Galea*)

them, and the fourth (a Ju 87) going to Johnston of No 126 Sqn.

On 29 March the remaining seven *Picket I* Spitfires were led in from *Eagle* by Battle of Britain ace Flt Lt R A 'Sailor' Barton. Also included in this group were future No 126 Sqn Malta aces Sgt P A 'Paddy' Schade and Australian Plt Off John Bisley.

In their first 20 days of operations, the Spitfires of No 249 Sqn and, from the 23rd, No 126 Sqn had accounted for 20 and one shared German aircraft destroyed for the loss of four Spitfires and their pilots in combat.

During the later part of March 1942, British 'Ultra' transcripts of German 'Enigma' signals traffic had noted the arrival in Rome of a senior German paratroop general and the transfer of paratroopers from the Russian front. The Luftwaffe's strength on Sicily was now at its peak, and Hitler had ordered Malta to be seized during April so as to bring to an end British interdiction of Axis supply lines in preparation for Rommel's coming North African offensive.

Despite the introduction of Spitfires, they had proven to be too few in number to effectively counter the 600+ German and Italian aircraft ranged against them. As March ended there was no respite for Malta's besieged garrison and civilian population. The island was warned – 'Invasion Imminent'.

HIGH HOPES AND DESPAIR

Notwithstanding the increasingly desperate plight of Malta, April at least started with a costly day of operations for the Luftwaffe. Nos 126 and 249 Sqns were now taking it in turns manning the limited number of Spitfires on alternate days, and on 1 April it was the latter unit's turn. A morning raid by 50 Ju 87s and Ju 88s, with fighter escorts, had attacked its targets unopposed, and No 249 Sqn's Spitfires finally went up at 1315 hrs. Six fighters intercepted four Bf 109s, and 'Johnny' Plagis (in AB335/GN-F) shot one of them down southeast of Grand Harbour. Shortly after the flight landed, four Spitfires were scrambled once again to intercept Ju 88s of I. and II./KG 77, and Plagis destroyed one and damaged another.

Flg Off Norman Lee was not so fortunate, however, as he was attacked by a Bf 109 and forced to crash-land at Takali with a shell splinter in his ankle. He was duly rushed off to hospital.

A Do 24 flying boat, with Bf 109 escort, was sent to search for downed pilots in the late afternoon. It soon attracted the attention of four Spitfires and a Hurricane. Amongst the No 249 Sqn pilots was 'Johnny' Plagis, who made good on his vow to avenge his friend Doug Leggo by shooting down another Bf 109 on his third sortie of the day. Also scoring his first Malta kill was New Zealander Sgt Ray Hesselyn, who knocked down a Messerschmitt fighter as well.

Yet another raid, consisting of 70 Axis aircraft (including 54 Stukas), was then detected approaching the dockyard and Hal Far. Five Spitfires intercepted the enemy dive-bombers, and Plt Off Peter Nash (in BP844/GN-W), Plagis (again in AB335/GN-F) and Sgt Hesselyn all destroyed a Stuka apiece – Nash had also downed a Ju 88 earlier in the day. Hesselyn later wrote about how he achieved his victories;

'We each got onto the tail of a bomber. Pete was slightly ahead of me, and I could see him firing before I opened up. His shells were striking, and suddenly his '87 blew up. I had no time to see any more. I was within 100 yards of my '87, and pressing the right gun button this time, I gave him everything I had. In a couple of seconds he burst into flames and dived into the drink.'

By the end of the day, 'Johnny' Plagis had been credited with four victories. These kills, added to the Stuka he had downed on the 25th, boosted his score to five confirmed, thus making him the first Spitfire ace of the siege of Malta. Plagis' feat of four in a day over Malta was matched only by Canadian ace George Beurling in late July.

The living conditions on Malta had come as a shock to the new pilots who had been posted in from fighter stations in the UK. Food was mainly bully beef, hot for breakfast and cold for lunch, with very little to accompany it, and as time went on there was less and less to go with this staple food. As things continued to deteriorate, officers were issued with the same rations as enlisted men.

The Axis bombing intensified during April, forcing pilots and other personnel to take shelter in slit trenches, sometimes for hours. Life became more hazardous and difficult. Transport, water supplies, electric power and telephone systems were constantly being interrupted, leaving frequent periods where there were no lights or radios. With the latter gone, Allied personnel and civilians alike missed daily BBC bulletins, and the cinemas closed, leading to an increased sense of isolation and desperation. Nerves were on edge, and everywhere servicemen and civilians were showing the strain. The Maltese appeared aged and haggard, as less and less of Valetta was left standing. Authorities set up communal feeding centres for civilians.

In May living conditions would deteriorate further, as food and water were stringently rationed. But haggard faces would break into smiles at the sight of RAF and Commonwealth personnel. The Maltese never failed to show their admiration for the young fighter pilots.

The latter often had to man their fighters on 'immediate readiness' as they attempted to counter Axis raids over the island. This meant sitting in

Spitfire VC BR190/2-A takes off in the company of an unknown No 249 Sqn aircraft during a scramble from Takali in late April. By this time BR190 had had two of its cannons removed, and was carrying the standard Spitfire VC armament of two 20mm cannon and four 0.303in machine guns. Although of poor quality, this photograph clearly shows that the Dark Blue/Grey paint on the fighter's uppersurfaces had been thinly applied – or perhaps not applied at all – around the fuselage roundels and code letters (*IWM*)

the cockpit in full flying kit, with helmet draped over the gunsight and a mechanic relaxing by the battery cart. It was often scorching hot in the cockpit, yet it would be freezing cold at 20,000 ft, so they had to wear a compromise kit – typically a shirt, 'Mae West', shorts, flying boots and gloves. On pre-dawn alert, the pilots were roused at 0330 hrs for a quick breakfast and a ride to the airfield. There they sat in their aircraft until 1300 hrs, when the next shift came on. If a call came through they were to be airborne in under a minute.

Raids went on unrelentingly through April, with the harbour and airfields being the target of waves of Stukas and Ju 88s. The latter typically came over 60 at a time, along with 20 Stukas and a large Bf 109 escort. Now a scramble of four Spitfires and six Hurricanes was considered an outstanding effort. AA guns were now also limited to 15 rounds a day. A number of bombing raids went uncontested, and victories for Hurricane and Spitfire pilots slowed to a trickle, as there simply were not enough serviceable fighters available to deal with the constant raids by the Luftwaffe.

A pattern had developed in which the Spitfires would climb high south of the island and then dive on the Luftwaffe formations over Malta. A pair of Hurricanes would then attempt to protect the Spitfires when they returned to base from marauding Bf 109s. Generally, there was no one to cover the Hurricanes when they landed.

On 8 April two Bf 109s and three Ju 88s were brought down, with one of the fighters being claimed by future ace Flg Off Ron West, but this was simply not enough to make inroads into the Axis effort.

Luftwaffe tactics at this point consisted of waves of bombers (generally 12 to 15 at a time) coming in from different heights and directions to hit

Spitfire VC BR226 is loaded aboard USS *Wasp* in Port Glasgow's King George V docks as part of Operation *Calendar*. As this photograph clearly shows, this aircraft (and the Spitfires parked behind it) were painted in factory-applied Desert colours of Middle Stone/Dark Earth and Sky Blue undersurfaces when they were embarked in the US Navy carrier. However, they were repainted en-route with various mixes of Blue-Grey. BR226 was the very machine in which Flt Lt Norman MacQueen met his death on 4 May 1942 (*via Frederick Galea*)

their targets, while the Bf 109s stayed aloft to gauge the scale of fighter reaction, before targeting the RAF units. Spitfire and Hurricane pilots had to fight their way up into the bomber formations, and then try to sneak by Bf 109 patrols waiting for them to return to base. The Luftwaffe could now boast 'Belagerung aus der Luft' (the siege from the air), as they bombed targets with impunity in the face of token opposition. Indeed, on 18 April, the Luftwaffe generated no fewer than 139 Ju 88 and 53 Ju 87 sorties against the various airfields on Malta, and not a single one was opposed by the RAF.

Numbers of available Spitfires on the island got a much needed boost two days later, however, when Operation *Calendar* was launched from the American aircraft carrier USS *Wasp*, sailing west of Malta. No fewer than 47 Spitfire VCs assigned to Nos 601 and 603 Sqns took off from the vessel, and all bar one of the fighters made it to Malta. The arrival of three squadrons worth of Spitfires injected new life into the island's thinly stretched defences, but the Luftwaffe immediately reacted by specifically targeting the fighters as they sat being re-armed and refuelled on the ground at Luqa and Takali.

By the morning of 21 April, only 27 of the newly arrived Spitfires remained airworthy, and by the end of that day the number had dropped to 17. The Germans also suffered significant losses during this period,

Repainted Spitfires of No 601 Sqn share deck space aboard *Wasp* with US Navy F4F-4 Wildcats from VF-71. Eleven of the Grumman fighters took off ahead of the Spitfires on 20 April 1942 to provide air cover for the task force at the start of Operation *Calendar*. Visible in this photograph wearing the livery code of the first flight of Spitfires off the carrier are BP975/1-O, BP954/1-D, BP975/1-K and 1-H/serial unknown. This group was led in to Luqa by No 601 Sqn's CO, Sqn Ldr John Bisdee (*via Frederick Galea*)

The pilot of Spitfire VC BR185/2-R runs up his engine prior to take-off as the fighter is wheeled into place on *Wasp*'s flightdeck on the morning of 20 April 1942. This aircraft was assigned to No 603 Sqn, whose Spitfires remained below deck until all the No 601 Sqn fighters had departed. They were then brought up to the flightdeck from the hangar deck one aircraft at a time on the carrier's elevator (seen here in the down position immediately behind BR185) (*via Frederick Galea*)

The second flight of Operation *Calendar*, consisting of No 603 Sqn in its entirety, begins the last leg of its journey to Malta. Spitfires visible in this photograph include BR117/2-X, BR183/2-D and 2-K/serial unknown. The unit was led in by Sqn Ldr Lord David Douglas-Hamilton in BR190/2-A (*via Frederick Galea*)

with No 249 Sqn alone claiming 16 victories between 20 and 22 April. Five Spitfire pilots were also killed during these ferocious clashes, with a further two being lost by month-end.

German units, supported by Italian fighters and bombers from 27 April onward, could absorb such casualties due to their large size, but the small RAF fighter force on Malta could not. As April ended, more Spitfires were urgently needed, and once again it would be up to *Wasp* to deliver them.

BACK FROM THE BRINK

The arrival of more Spitfires was still some nine days away when Flt Lt Norman MacQueen and Plt Off Les Watts of No 249 Sqn claimed the first kill of the new month by sharing in the destruction of a Bf 109 from 6./JG 53 during the morning of 1 May. Honours were evened up that afternoon, however, as New Zealander Flt Sgt Jack Rae was shot down in No 603 Sqn Spitfire BP962/2-R by a 6./JG 53 machine while attempting to intercept Italian Z.1007bis bombers. Despite having been wounded in the leg, Rae successfully baled out and came down near Rabat. He spent a month recovering in hospital, after which he joined No 249 Sqn.

With two kills to his name from a previous tour on the Channel Front with No 485 Sqn, Rae scored 4.5 victories (as well as three and one shared probables and five damaged) while on Malta. Returning to No 485 Sqn in May 1943, he claimed a further 5.5 kills prior to being forced to bale out of his Spitfire IX over France when its engine failed on 22 August 1943. He spent the rest of the war as a PoW.

The loss of yet another Spitfire meant that the fighter squadrons could now only put up a token defence against Axis raids. Nevertheless, Plt Off Nash claimed a Bf 109 destroyed for his sixth kill on 3 May. The following afternoon, five Z.1007s, escorted by five C.202s and ten Bf 109Fs, bombed shipping in Grand Harbour. Eight Spitfires were scrambled, four each from Nos 249 and 601 Sqns, and an aircraft from the latter unit subsequently crash-landed at Luqa after its radiator had been holed by one of the Messerschmitts.

Leading the aircraft from No 249 Sqn was Flt Lt Norman MacQueen, and the formation included Sgt Paul Brennan. Having arrived too late to engage the Italian bombers, the Spitfires were bounced by the Bf 109s. Following a series of violent manoeuvres, Brennan succeeded in downing

Australian Flt Sgt Paul Brennan of No 249 Sqn used BR190/2-A to down a Bf 109 on 4 May 1942 for his sixth victory. BR190 was carrying standard Spitfire VC armament of two 20mm cannon in the inboard position and four 0.303in machine guns at the time of Brennan's success (*IWM*)

Spitfire VC BR187/2-G was a typical No 603 Sqn Operation *Calendar* Spitfire. It featured *Wasp* Blue-Grey uppersurfaces, with the Desert colours left around the serial number, and Sky Blue undersides. The fighter was used by Flt Lt William Douglas to damage a Bf 109 on 3 May, but was crashed by Sgt J W Connell of No 601 Sqn the very next day and declared a write-off on the 6th (*IWM*)

Performing a low-level pass for the benefit of a newsreel camera, Spitfire VC BR187/2-G buzzes Takali airfield. By now sporting standard Spitfire VC armament, BR187, like many of the *Calendar* aircraft, had a short wartime career, being written off on 6 May (*IWM*)

a German fighter (for his sixth kill) after the latter overshot him.

During the same dogfight, Flt Lt MacQueen failed to hear radio calls (due to R/T inoperability) warning him of impending danger as two Bf 109s from III./JG 53 bounced him from above. The first enemy fighter overshot him, but the second one, flown by Unteroffizier Walter Manz, pulled up beneath MacQueen's Spitfire (BR226) and fired a quick snapshot into the underside of its fuselage. Sgt Brennan subsequently recalled;

'As I watched, MacQueen's aircraft gave a sudden lurch, side-slipped about 1000 ft, and then seemed to come under control again. I did not like the look of things. I called up, "Mac, if you're not okay for God's sake bale out. I will cover you.' There was no reply. A few minutes later his aircraft gave another lurch, went into a vertical dive, and crashed at Naxxar, a mile from the aerodrome.'

Witnesses thought that MacQueen had been seriously wounded by the attack, and had eventually loss control of his aircraft. Inexperienced American pilot Plt Off Fred Almos had been his wingman on this mission, and there was a general consensus that he had been too close to protect MacQueen's tail. Almos was subsequently transferred to the newly formed all-American flight within No 126 Sqn. The well-liked and popular Norman MacQueen was posthumously awarded the DFC, with his final tally standing at seven and two shared kills and four and four shared damaged. He was the first Spitfire ace to lose his life in the defence of Malta.

Another Spitfire (BR116/V) was shot down in flames over Hal Far on 6 May when it was hit by three cannon shells fired from a Bf 109. Flt Lt H A S Johnston of No 126 Sqn baled out with shell splinters in his legs and serious burns to his face and arms.

The following day, numerous patrols were made by C.202s along Malta's west coast in anticipation of the arrival of the reinforcing flights of Spitfires from *Wasp*. The Italian intelligence service had picked up

word about the fighters' imminent arrival, but had got its dates wrong. The Luftwaffe initiated a new offensive against Malta on 8 May, and again the *Regia Aeronautica* was much to the fore. Three Bf 109s were shot down during the first raid of the day, two of which fell to Plt Off Reade Tilley for his first kills.

Floridian Tilley was a key member of No 126 Sqn's American flight. Having made one damaged claim while flying with No 121 Sqn on the Channel front, he was sent to Malta with No 601 Sqn and claimed a Bf 109 damaged with this unit on 28 April. Tilley then transferred to No 126 Sqn. By 23 May he had 'made ace' and been awarded a DFC.

The second raid of 8 May went unopposed, as there were now only 12 Spitfires and Hurricanes left serviceable on Malta, and these were being held back for the pending arrival of the reinforcing flight of Spitfires from *Wasp* the following day. On a more positive note, the awarding of a DFC to Flg Off McNair and DFMs to Sgts Brennan and Hesselyn was announced on the 8th. All three men had achieved ace status in the defence of Malta.

WASP STINGS TWICE

The carriers *Wasp* and *Eagle* had departed Gibraltar on the night of 7/8 May, the vessels carrying 50 and 17 Spitfire Vs, respectively, in an operation codenamed *Bowery*. The first two flights were to be led off *Eagle* by No 249 Sqn veterans Sqn Ldr Stan Grant and Flt Lt Ron West, with the three remaining flights off the British carrier being headed up by 'Laddie' Lucas, Raoul Daddo-Langlois and 'Buck' McNair.

American Plt Off Reade Tilley arrived on Malta with No 601 Sqn as part of Operation *Calendar* on 20 April. His previous spell in the frontline with No 121 'Eagle' Sqn on the Channel Front prepared him well for combat in the central Mediterranean, as he quickly claimed a series of kills once he had joined No 126 Sqn's American flight in early May. Achieving ace status on 23 May, Tilley was awarded a DFC at this time as a result of his numerous aerial successes (*via Reade Tilley*)

Spitfire BP965/4-C takes off from *Wasp* during the morning of 9 May 1942 as part of Operation *Bowery*. All Spitfires departing the carrier were identifiable by either a '3' or '4' in combination with a letter. It appears that the Spitfires on *Eagle* featured the code letter 'C' followed by a number. Some of these machines were issued to No 249 Sqn, which recorded having operated Spitfires BR107/C-22, BR108/C-20 and BR109/C-30. This peculiar coding system is thought to have also been used in Operation *LB*, and certainly during *Style* (*via Frederick Galea*)

Spitfire VC BP845 is seen on a barge in Port Glasgow prior to being loaded aboard *Eagle* as part of Operation *Calendar*. After the first flight of Spitfires arrived on Malta in early March 1942, it has been widely reported by survivors such as 'Buck' McNair, Denis Barnham and others that further shipments of fighters during the siege usually had their uppersurfaces repainted Blue/Blue-Grey. The ideal choice for the job was Dark Mediterranean Blue, with Light Mediterranean Blue and Extra Dark Sea Grey being available too. Eyewitness accounts also reveal that there was much mixing and thinning down of paint prior to its application (*via Frederick Galea*)

History in the making. Having been previously launched from *Wasp*, Spitfire BR126/3-X returns to the carrier to perform the first deck landing ever made by a Spitfire. The aircraft's pilot, Canadian Plt Off Jerry Smith, was forced to turn back on 9 May when his fuel tank pump went unserviceable. He was faced with the choice of either ditching or trying to land back aboard *Wasp*, thus saving a valuable Spitfire. Having chosen the latter option, he is seen here making his final approach over the carrier's stern (*via Frederick Galea*)

The first of the 64 aircraft despatched from the carriers (three were left behind due to their unserviceability) took off shortly after dawn on 9 May. Tragedy struck when the 23rd Spitfire to leave *Wasp* failed to gain sufficient flying speed due to its propeller being incorrectly set in coarse pitch. The fighter crashed into the sea and was cut in two by the bow of the carrier, killing Canadian pilot Sgt R D Sherrington.

Fellow Canadian pilot Plt Off Jerry Smith suffered a faulty fuel tank pump in his aircraft (BR126/3-X) and decided to risk landing his valuable Spitfire back aboard *Wasp*. He pulled his fighter up with only 6ft of flight-deck left, despite his Spitfire lacking an arrester hook. Two aircraft went missing en route to Malta, but the remaining 60 landed safely at Takali and Luqa between 1030 hrs and 1100 hrs.

Following the previous month's fiasco in the wake of Operation *Calendar*, where German attacks on Maltese airfields had been carefully timed to coincide with the arrival of the new fighters, a plan had been

31

hatched by Wg Cdr 'Jumbo' Gracie that would ensure the hasty turn-around of the new Spitfires once they were on the ground at Takali, Luqa and, for the first time, Hal Far. Pilots had been briefed on what aircraft pens they were to taxi to, these being clearly marked with the code of each particular aircraft. Again, all Spitfires had been repainted prior to take-off with dark Blue-Grey paint, and the aircraft were marked with either a '3' or a '4' on their fuselage, with the individual code letter forward of the roundel. This in turn corresponded with a specific aircraft pen on the island.

Five groundcrewmen per pen were waiting to remove the long-range tanks and then refuel and service the Spitfires as soon as they had landed on Malta, the fuel for each individual fighter being kept in 4-gallon cans, protected by sandbags, within each pen. Finally, no matter how senior the rank of the pilot who had made the ferry flight, the Malta pilot in the pen was in command, and he would take over the Spitfire at once and get it back into the air as quickly as possible. This would pre-vent the precious fighter from being caught on the ground by the Luftwaffe. Gracie had stated that he wanted every Spitfire airborne again within 15 minutes of its landing on the island.

A relieved Plt Off Jerry Smith smiles for the camera immediately after landing on *Wasp*. His fighter had come to a stop with just 6ft of flightdeck left to spare! (*via Frederick Galea*)

And these measure paid off, for despite the fact that there were nine separate Axis air raids that day, only four Spitfires had been shot down as they attempted to defend the three airfields from attack. A further six had been damaged on the ground.

Amongst the quartet of pilots killed was Australian Hurricane ace Plt Off G R Tweedale of No 185 Sqn, who was shot down during his very first flight in a Spitfire (BR248) by Leutnant Erich Beckmann of III./JG 53. He had arrived on Malta on 22 February 1942, and claimed seven destroyed (including two on 8 May), two probables and two damaged prior to his death. Fellow Australian Flt Lt Ray Sly, who had just flown in from *Wasp*, died when his fighter (BR348) clipped the top of a dispersal pen at Hal Far as he attempted to take-off down-wind to help defend the airfield.

Despite these losses, 11 German and Italian aircraft had been destroyed by RAF fighters, some of which had fallen to newly re-equipped No 185 Sqn. A number of the *Bowery* aircraft had been given to the veteran Hurricane unit at Hal Far as replacements for its dwindling fleet of

Wasp's highly experienced Landing Signals Officer who guided Smith back aboard ship was none other than future ranking US Navy ace Lt Cdr David McCampbell. Smith had only been briefed on how to take-off during his brief time on *Wasp*, and therefore did not understand US Navy deck landing 'etiquette'. In this photograph, McCampbell has just said to Smith, 'I take my hat off to you!' His younger brother Roderick Smith, who later became an ace on Malta, commented after the war that this was his favourite photograph of his brother. It was the last one taken prior to his landing on Malta, and before the effects of constant hunger and intense action set in. Jerry Smith was killed in combat on 10 August 1942, flying Spitfire BR366 (*via Frederick Galea*)

Hawker fighters. Future squadron ace Flt Sgt J W 'Slim' Yarra described his first use of the Spitfire on 9 May:

'At 1400 hrs our first scramble in Spitfires took place when a section of four took off, led by Flt Lt R M Lloyd. The boys got in amongst the bombers – Ju 87s and Ju 88s – and there was a lot of squirting and carrying on for a while. Plt Off Ernie Broad (BR294/GL-E) got one Ju 87 probably destroyed and a second one damaged. For once the sky was full of friendly aircraft. There were Spitfires everywhere.'

Twenty-four hours after the Spitfires were flown in, the fast minelayer-cruiser HMS *Welshman* completed its unescorted run from Gibraltar by slipping quietly into Grand Harbour just before dawn. Its cargo consisted of much needed AA ammunition, foodstuffs, aero engines and 100 RAF technicians to aid in the servicing of the additional fighters now on the island. These groundcrew had arrived just in time to witness what would prove to be the climax of the Axis bombing offensive against Malta. Indeed, the aerial action of 10 May 1942 has gone down in history as the turning point in the air battle for the island.

The arrival of *Welshman* and the Spitfires provoked an intense reaction from the Luftwaffe and the *Regia Aeronautica*. Apart from two early morning reconnaissance sorties, there was no Axis activity until 1020 hrs. At that time, a raid consisting of 20 Ju 87s and 10 Ju 88s, escorted by Bf 109s from JG 53, approached the harbour heading for the cruiser. No fewer than 37 Spitfires and 13 Hurricanes rose to intercept the German aircraft, taking the Luftwaffe by surprise. All bombs missed their target thanks to the Spitfires of Nos 126, 185, 249, 601 and 603 Sqns and a very effective smoke screen generated by smoke canisters delivered by *Welshman*. Weighing into the action with No 249 Sqn, Plt Off Peter Nash observed:

'Terrific party over Grand Harbour. All the Ju 87s missed the target. Everyone got something. The Stukas stuck! Starboard wing came off one and the other disappeared into the smoke screen at 200 ft!'

Nash was credited with destroying two Ju 87s whilst flying BR108/2-C. Veteran No 185 Sqn Hurricane pilot, and future ace, Australian Sgt Tony Boyd, flying Spitfire BR350/3-J, described the action from his perspective:

'The most terrific air battle ever seen here – astounding – plus an appalling barrage. There were

Typical of the Operation *Bowery* Spitfires, this aircraft appears to have been painted in a lighter shade than the *Calendar* fighters. Their Desert colours were overpainted in Gibraltar, mostly in Blue-Grey mixes. They also appear to have been painted with spray guns, revealing a slight overspray between the top and bottom colours. Most had the uppersurface camouflage extended down the sides of the tropical air-filter, leaving only the very bottom in Sky Blue (*via Frederick Galea*)

A No 249 Sqn Spitfire is refuelled at Takali, the fighter having been repainted in a Blue-Grey shade. This shot shows the overpaint of the leading edge of the wing – more typical on US Navy aircraft. Although overpainting such as this originated on *Wasp*, it was carried over well into 1943 on Malta Spitfires that had never been on the vessel. Note the swastika on the fuel bowser! (*via Frederick Galea*)

33

about 25 Spits, eight Hurris, 30 Stukas, 15 Ju 88s and 20 Me 109s all mixed up in one enormous milling fight. Thirty enemy aircraft destroyed or damaged in this raid. We lost one Spit. I got a Ju 88 probable and a Ju 88 damaged. First one at 2000–3000 ft over Grand Harbour with a five-second burst. Second at 300–200 yards, with a large explosion in rear of cabin – black smoke poured out and it nosed down in shallow dive three miles north of Grand Harbour.'

A soldier, a sailor and an airman carry out the refuelling and re-arming of a Spitfire VC of No 603 Sqn in a makeshift revetment at Takali in May 1942. Note that the aircraft has had its inner 20mm cannon removed and the gun ports filled with locally made wooden bungs. Its outer 0.303in machine guns also appear to have been removed (*via Bruce Robertson*)

Apparently pausing to lick its wounds, the Luftwaffe returned at 1400 hrs, sending over seven Ju 88s, covered by about 30 Bf 109s, to again attack Grand Harbour. This time 20 Spitfires and six Hurricanes rose to intercept, and again all bombs dropped missed *Welshman*. Finally, at 1740 hrs, a third raid headed for the harbour comprised of five Z.1007bis and escorting C.202s and Re.2001s (the latter making their operational début), followed by more Ju 87s, Ju 88s and Bf 109s. A total of 42 Spitfires rose to intercept from all five Spitfire squadrons, and again the Axis fliers received a bloody nose.

Amongst the No 603 Sqn pilots involved was future ace Flg Off Richard 'Mitch' Mitchell, flying as wingman to Flt Lt Bill Douglas (who also 'made ace' later in the war). Mitchell described his first kill as follows:

'Bill dived down into the barrage and I followed close on him. We flew three times to and fro in the barrage, trusting to luck to avoid the flak. Then I spotted a Ju 87 climbing out at the fringe of the barrage and I turned and chased him. I gave him a one-second burst of cannon and he broke off sharply to the left. At that moment another Ju 87 came up in front of my nose and I turned and chased him and let him have it. His engine started to pour out black smoke and he started weaving. I kept the tit pressed hard, and after a further burst of two to three seconds with the one cannon I had left – the other one had jammed – he keeled over at 1500 ft and went into the drink.'

Mitchell also damaged a Bf 109 in this engagement.

Spitfire pilots ultimately claimed nine Ju 87s, six Ju 88s, three Bf 109s, one Z.1007bis and one C.202 destroyed, and the AA gunners were credited with downing five Ju 87s, one Ju 88 and one Bf 109. Actual Luftwaffe losses to all causes amounted to five Ju 88s, four Ju 87s and three Bf 109s, whilst the Italians did indeed have a Z.1007bis and a C.202 destroyed.

In return, No 601 Sqn had Australian Plt Off G M Briggs killed in action, and two other Spitfires were shot down (one by a direct hit from an AA shell) but both pilots survived.

Gone were the days of putting up a token defence of four or, at best, six Spitfires and a similar number of Hurricanes. Some 110 Spitfire sorties had been flown on 10 May, backed up by 14 Hurricane sorties. And such a response had resulted in the destruction of a significant number of enemy aircraft. The recovery of Allied air supremacy over

'Paddy' Schade, who was born in Malta to a Dutch father and Irish mother, joined the RAF in 1940 and was initially posted to No 501 Sqn, before being transferred to No 54 Sqns. In early 1942 he received orders sending him to Malta, and he flew a replacement Spitfire to the island from *Eagle* on 29 March. Joining No 126 Sqn, Schade claimed a Ju 87 destroyed and one shared on 23 April for his first kills. He took part in the ferocious aerial battles of 9–10 May, destroying two Z.1007bis, a Ju 88. Between 15 June and 11 July Schade was credited with the destruction of seven Bf 109s and a C.202, thus making him Malta's then top ace with 13.5 confirmed victories. Sent back to the UK in August, whereupon he received a DFM, Schade eventually returned to frontline flying with No 91 Sqn in October 1943. He added 3.5 V1s to his score prior to being killed in a mid-air collision with a Tempest V whilst pursuing another flying bomb on 31 July 1944 (*via Frederick Galea*)

Malta had begun in earnest, and although much hard fighting still lay ahead for the island's air defence squadrons, the corner had been turned.

Amongst the pilots to claim victories on the 10th were the following aces – Peck, Goldsmith and Schade of No 126 Sqn, Nash, Brennan, Plagis, Grant and Hesselyn of No 249 Sqn, and Bisdee of No 601 Sqn. Flt Sgt 'Paddy' Schade's Ju 88 kill was particularly significant for it took his tally to 5.5 victories.

Born in Malaya to a Dutch father and Irish mother, Schade had joined the RAF in 1940. After serving with Nos 501 and 54 Sqns in 1941, he received orders to Malta and flew a Spitfire off *Eagle* on 29 March 1942 as part of *Picket II*. Upon his arrival on the island, Schade joined No 126 Sqn, which was alternating every other day with No 249 Sqn for use of the limited number of Spitfires then available. He soon began scoring, with a Ju 87 destroyed and one shared on 23 April. Schade took part in the crucial air battles on 9 and 10 May, downing two Z.1007bis and a Ju 88 during this critical 48-hour period to make ace.

REDUCED THREAT

Amazingly, despite the reversals of 10 May, Feldmarschall Kesselring formed the erroneous opinion that the island of Malta was no longer a threat, informing Hitler that the Luftwaffe had prevailed and only modest losses had been suffered by German units. In actuality, the continuous operations against Malta had kept 350 to 450 Luftwaffe aircraft heavily engaged at a time when they could have been operating elsewhere on the Eastern Front or in North Africa. Losses had in fact been high, and in May 1942 alone 259 Luftwaffe aircraft had been destroyed or damaged on operations against Malta.

Following his communiqués with Berlin, Kesselring was ordered in mid-May to reduce the intensity of air operations against Malta and run down the German presence on Sicily. I./JG 3 and II./JG 53 duly left for Russia, III./JG 53, III./StG 3, III./ZG 26 and I./ NJG 2 were sent to North Africa and I./KG 54 headed for Greece.

These transfers did not take place until mid- to late May, however. In the meantime, there was still plenty of fighting to be done by the defenders of Malta.

On 11 May, the Luftwaffe took a back seat to the efforts of the *Regia Aeronautica*, whose fighters were out early looking for survivors from the mauling of the previous evening. At 0725 hrs, Re.2001s of the newly arrived 2° *Gruppo* (misidentified by RAF pilots as C.202s) encountered a section of No 249 Sqn fighters, and Plt Off 'Johnny' Plagis (in Spitfire 3-N) claimed to have downed one through sheer intimidation:

'I flew straight at the nearest machine, with the intention of ramming it. I did not fire a shot, but the Macchi pilot, suddenly realising his number might be up too, took violent evasive action, stalled and crashed into the sea.'

Credited with a confirmed victory, Plagis was now Malta's highest-scoring Spitfire pilot, with seven and one shared kill to his name. He maintained that position until about 1030 hrs that morning. At that time a raid of 15 Ju 88s and 40 Bf 109s approached Malta, and now flying Plagis' lucky 3-N, Sgt Paul Brennan downed a Bf 109 to take his tally to

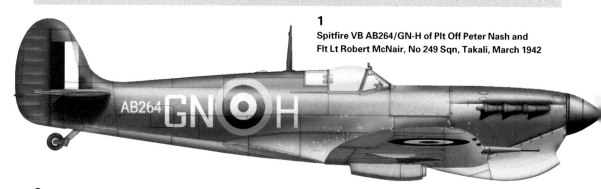

1

Spitfire VB AB264/GN-H of Plt Off Peter Nash and
Flt Lt Robert McNair, No 249 Sqn, Takali, March 1942

2

Spitfire VB AB451/GN-T of Flg Off George Buchanan,
No 249 Sqn, Takali, 1 April 1942

3

Spitfire VC BP964/1-X of Sgt Adrian Goldsmith RAAF,
No 126 Sqn, Luqa, April 1942

4

Spitfire VC BP962/2-R of Flt Lt William Douglas,
No 603 Sqn, Takali, April 1942

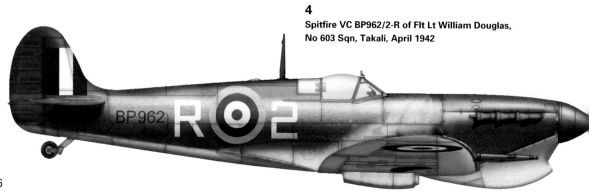

5
Spitfire VC BR190/2-A of Flt Sgt Paul Brennan RAAF,
No 249 Sqn, Takali, April–May 1942

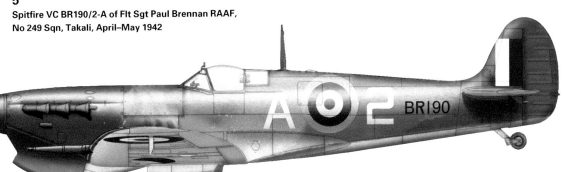

6
Spitfire VC BR195/1-Q of Plt Off Peter Nash,
No 249 Sqn, Takali, 16 May 1942

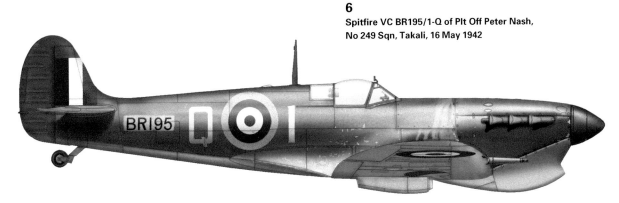

7
Spitfire VC serial unknown/U of Flt Lt Denis
Barnham, No 601 Sqn, Luqa, 14 May 1942

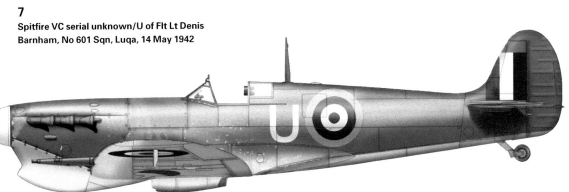

8
Spitfire VC BP975/1-K of Flt Lt Denis Barnham,
No 601 Sqn, Luqa, 24 April 1942

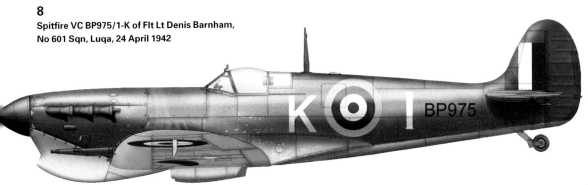

9
Spitfire VC BR107/C-22 of Plt Off Peter Nash,
No 249 Sqn, Takali, May 1942

10
Spitfire VC BR126/3-X of Plt Off Jerry Smith RCAF,
No 126 Sqn, Luqa, 9 May 1942

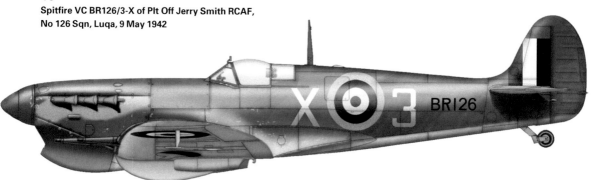

11
Spitfire VC BR187/2-G of Flt Lt William Douglas,
No 603 Sqn, Takali, 3 May 1942

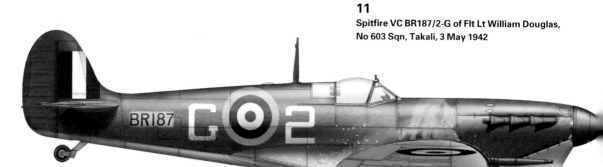

12
Spitfire VC BR290/1-T of Sgt Adrian Goldsmith RAAF,
No 126 Sqn, Luqa, 14 May 1942

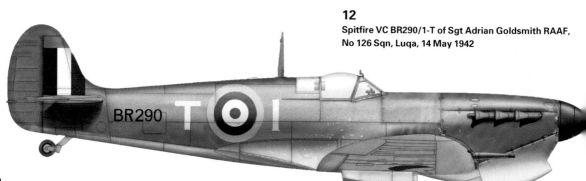

13
Spitfire VC BR294/GL-E of Sgt Wilbert Dodd RCAF,
No 185 Sqn, Hal Far, 22 May 1942

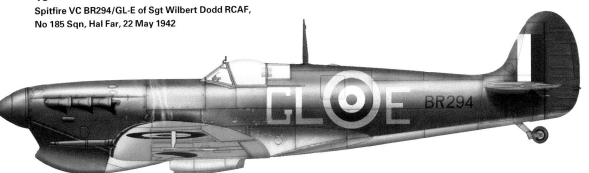

14
Spitfire VC BR349/3-C of Sgt Tony Boyd RAAF,
No 185 Sqn, Hal Far, 14 May 1942

15
Spitfire VC BR246/B of Plt Off Frank Jones RCAF,
No 249 Sqn, Takali, 6 June 1942

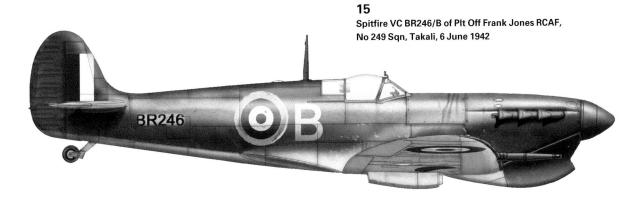

16
Spitfire VC serial unknown/UF-M of Plt Off Bruce
Ingram RNZAF, No 601 Sqn, Luqa, 15 June 1942

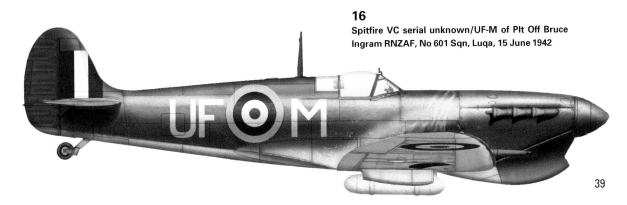

17
Spitfire VC BR321/GL-J of Flt Lt 'Johnny' Plagis, No 185
Sqn, Hal Far, 6–7 June 1942

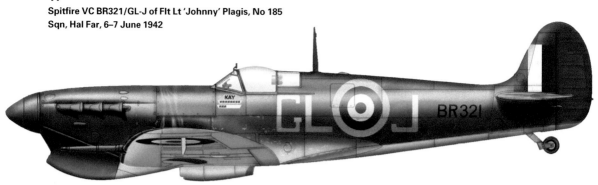

18
Spitfire VC BR387/GL-W of Plt Off John 'Slim' Yarra RAAF,
No 185 Sqn, Hal Far, July 1942

19
Spitfire VB BR562/X-R of Flt Lt Ray Hesselyn
RNZAF, No 249 Sqn, Takali, July 1942

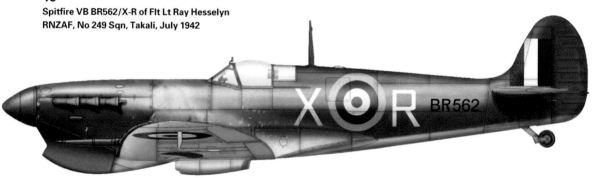

20
Spitfire VC BR295/T-H of Plt Off Lawrence Verrall
RNZAF, No 249 Sqn, Takali, 27 June 1942

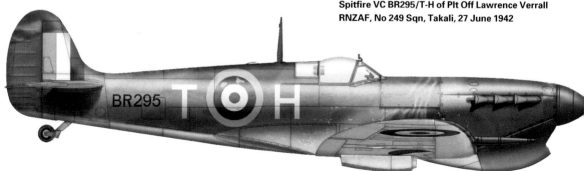

21
Spitfire VC BP989/4-N of Flg Off Wally McLeod RCAF,
No 603 Sqn, Takali, 9 July 1942

22
Spitfire VC serial unknown/N-MK of Flt Sgt 'Paddy' Schade,
No 126 Sqn, Luqa, 9 July 1942

23
Spitfire VC BR130/T-D of Sgt George Beurling,
No 249 Sqn, Takali, 14 July 1942

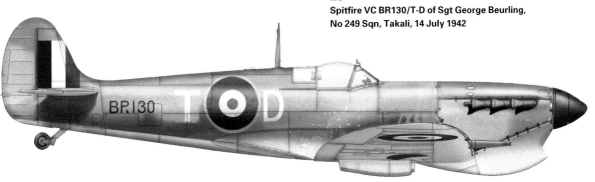

24
Spitfire VC BP952/F-MK of Plt Off Rod Smith RCAF,
No 126 Sqn, Luqa, July 1942

25
Spitfire VB EN976/T-C of Plt Off John McElroy RCAF,
No 249 Sqn, Takali, July 1942

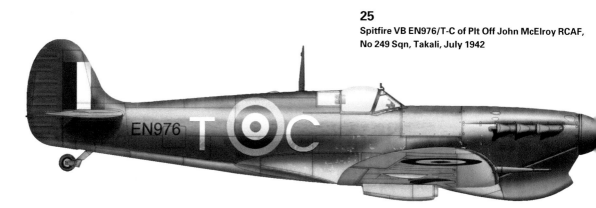

26
Spitfire VC BP869/T-K of Sgt Vasseure Wynn RCAF,
No 249 Sqn, Takali, 28 July 1942

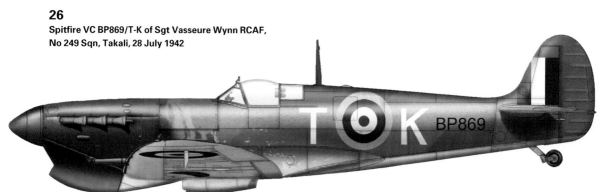

27
Spitfire VC BR301/UF-S of Plt Off John McElroy RCAF,
No 249 Sqn, Takali, July 1942

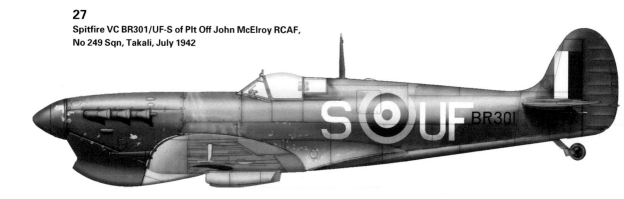

28
Spitfire VC BR375/GL-A of Plt Off Gray Stenborg RNZAF,
No 185 Sqn, Hal Far, June 1942

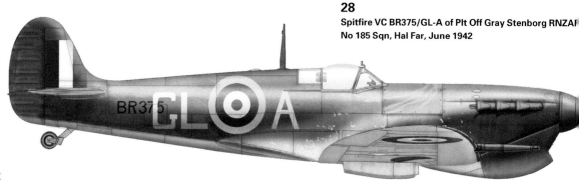

29
Spitfire VB EP200/GL-T of Flt Sgt Colin Parkinson RAAF,
No 603 Sqn, Takali, July 1942

30
Spitfire VB EP706/T-L of Plt Off George Beurling,
No 249 Sqn, Takali, October 1942

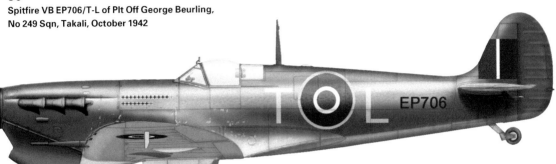

31
Spitfire VC BR112/X of Sgt Claude Weaver
RCAF, No 185 Sqn, Hal Far, 9 September 1942

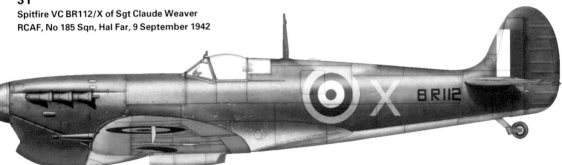

32
Spitfire VB EP691/X-A of Plt Off Colin Parkinson
RAAF, No 229 Sqn, Takali, October 1942

33
Spitfire VB EP717/D-v of Flt Sgt Ian Maclennan RCAF,
No 1435 Sqn, Luqa, 11 October 1942

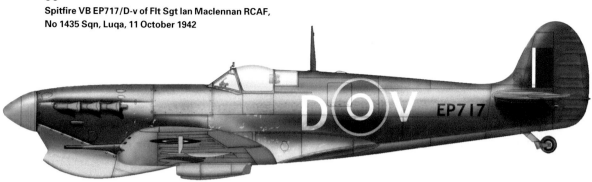

34
Spitfire VC BR311/L-MK of Flt Lt William
Johnson, No 126 Sqn, Takali, July 1942

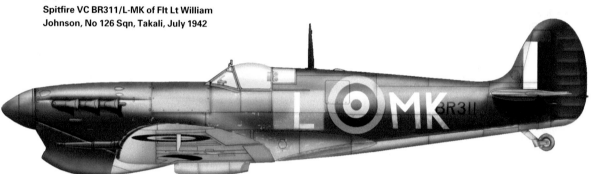

35
Spitfire VC BR379/T-V of Sgt Tommy Parks,
No 249 Sqn, Takali, July 1942

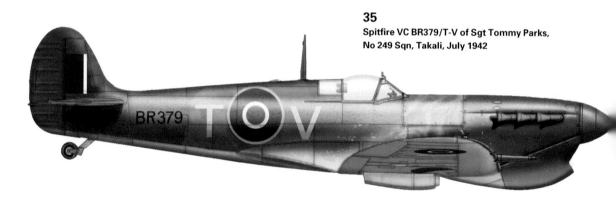

36
Spitfire VC AR560/JM-T of Wg Cdr John
Thompson, Luqa Wing, Luqa, April 1943

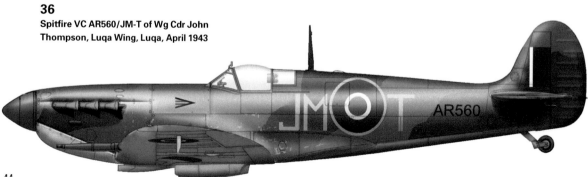

37
Spitfire VC BR498/PP-H of Wg Cdr Peter Prosser Hanks,
Luqa Wing, Luqa, October 1942

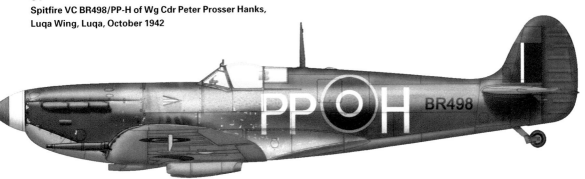

38
Spitfire VB EP829/T-N of Sqn Ldr John J Lynch RCAF,
No 249 Sqn, Krendi, April 1943

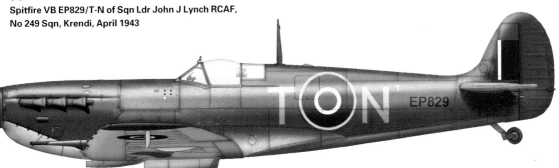

39
Spitfire VC AB535/T-Z of Flg Off 'Hap' Kennedy RCAF,
No 249 Sqn, Krendi, April 1943

40
Spitfire VB EP606/X-P of Flg Off Ryan Gosling
RCAF, No 229 Sqn, Krendi, April 1943

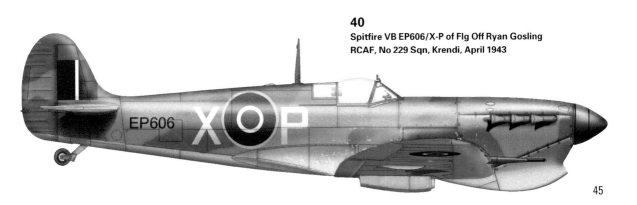

There are no known photos of an actual dogfight taking place over Malta. This scratchboard illustration by the prolific artist, and No 601 Sqn ace, Flt Lt Denis Barnham shows his impression of just such an engagement with Bf 109s during the spring and summer of 1942 (*via Frederick Galea*)

eight. Minutes later, Plt Off Peter Nash (flying BR107/C-22) destroyed another Messerschmitt fighter for his eighth kill, thus equalling Brennan's total.

No 603 Sqn's Flt Lt Douglas also destroyed a Bf 109 that afternoon, but he was in turn forced to bale out after his Spitfire (BP964) was hit by Plt Off R Bairnsfather (in BP991). Both aircraft were lost, although the pilots survived with minor injuries.

Five more Spitfires were written off and two pilots killed during a series of clashes on 12 May. A number of enemy aircraft were destroyed in return, however, with Kiwi ace Sgt Ray Hesselyn downing a Bf 109 that had just sent Plt Off Bert Mitchell of No 603 Sqn crashing to his death (in BR127). Hesselyn was again in the thick of things the following day, when 16 Ju 87s of III./StG 3 returned to Malta for the first time since the *Gruppe*'s mauling over Grand Harbour three days earlier. A total of 26 Bf 109s escorted the dive-bombers, which targeted Hal Far shortly after midday.

Eight Spitfires from No 249 Sqn intercepted the German raiders, and Hesselyn downed two Bf 109s in quick succession. Three victories in two days had taken the New Zealander's tally to nine, thus making him the new Spitfire top scorer. He had shot the second fighter off the tail of future ace Flt Lt Ronnie West, whose voice then came over the R/T loud and clear. 'Spit that just shot down that '109. Thanks a hell of a lot!'

Hesselyn's hot scoring streak continued on the 14th, when Axis aircraft again focused their attention on Maltese airfields. A series of raids were made, with the attacking formation typically consisting of three or four bombers, escorted by large numbers of fighters. The first raid, comprising three Ju 88s of KGr 806 and a handful of Bf 109 *Jabos*, protected by more Messerschmitt fighters, headed for Takali and Luqa at 0900 hrs. Whilst opposing this attack, Hesselyn became the first Malta Spitfire pilot to reach double figures when he downed a Ju 88:

'I got on the tail of my Ju 88, closed to about 50 yards and opened fire. I could see three members of the crew in the glasshouse, as well as the rear gunner, who had already opened fire at me. I gave it everything I had, and I saw my shells strike along the Ju 88's fuselage and smack into the glasshouse. It was still carrying its bomb-load, and when the ordnance was hit the aircraft blew up.'

Hesselyn's flight commander, Flt Lt West, was also credited with the destruction of a Ju 88, but it appears that he had also attacked the bomber downed by the Kiwi ace. Several other aces also claimed victories during the course of the day, including Australian J L 'Tony' Boyd. Having flown Hurricanes in the defence of Malta since January 1942 with Nos 242 and 185 Sqns, he downed the Bf 109 of 4./JG 53's Leutnant Alfred Hammer while flying BR349/C-3. This success took Boyd's tally to five and two shared destroyed.

At 1200 hrs three more Ju 88s approached Takali, again with a large fighter escort of Bf 109s, C.202s and Re.2001s. Flt Sgt D L Ferraby and Sgt Boyd went after eight C.202s, which were soon joined by a number of Re.2001s. Ferraby hit one of the Macchis, but Boyd's fighter (BR349/C) was seen to spin out of the dogfight and crash onto the airfield at Takali. A popular and cheerful personality who was considered to be the doyen of Hurricane pilots, Boyd was just days away from ending his tour when he was killed.

Flt Lt Denis Barnham in his famous 'white spots' Spitfire VC. To aid his flight in forming up on him when in the air, he had white spots added to the wingtips of his aircraft, as seen in this photo. Barnham also had his canopy removed (although it was still clearly in place when this photograph was taken). His CO, Sqn Ldr John Bisdee ordered that the canopy be immediately reinstated following Barnham's brush with death on 14 May 1942. The spots were also painted out after this sortie, as they seemed to attract every enemy fighter in the sky (*IWM*)

A late afternoon raid consisting of three Ju 88s from KGr 806, as well as a large fighter escort, was targeted by 26 Spitfires of Nos 249, 126 and 601 Sqns. Future ace Flt Lt Denis Barnham led in a section of Spitfires from the latter unit, the wingtips of his Spitfire (serial unknown) having been decorated with a single white spot so as to enable his section to recognise his fighter quickly in the air. After a hair-raising dogfight in which he destroyed one of the aforementioned Ju 88s and claimed a Bf 109 probable, his white-spotted Spitfire attracted the attention of five more enemy fighters, and they chased him all the way back to his airfield at Luqa.

Barnham's CO, Spitfire ace Sqn Ldr John Bisdee (who had been shot down and wounded shortly after flying to Malta from *Wasp* on 20 April), ordered him to replace his fighter's hood, which Barnham had had removed to allow clearer vision. He did not have to be told to have the white spots painted out:

'I apologised to "Chiefy" for all the extra trouble I'd caused him. He smiled back at me with such a patient, kindly, understanding. I'm still shaken up after that trip.'

The Spitfire pilots had claimed seven Ju 88s and five Bf 109s on 14 May, but these successes had cost the lives of long-serving No 185 Sqn pilots Sgts Colin Finlay and Tony Boyd (both of whom were due to leave the island on the 17th), as well as American Flt Sgt Harry Fox of No 249

47

Sqn – he was the second 'Harry' Fox to be lost by the unit since its arrival on Malta.

No 603 Sqn's Sgt Yarra was credited with two of the three C.202s destroyed on 15 May, his first victim colliding with his wingman, thus doubling the Australian's tally. He would 'make ace' with two Bf 109 claims three days later.

More victories came on the 16th, with perhaps the most significant being the 10./JG 53 Bf 109F *Jabo* that was shared by Plt Offs Plagis (BR176/C-25) and Nash (BR195), which the latter pilot described in

his logbook as 'the 100th enemy aircraft destroyed on Malta by No 249 Sqn'. Less than 24 hours after writing this entry, Malta's then ranking Spitfire ace was dead.

The morning of 17 May had started promisingly enough for No 249 Sqn when Flg Off Buchanan (who had 'made ace' the previous day by destroying a C.202 in the same action that had brought the unit's its century) downed a reconnaissance Ju 88D of 1(F)./122 at 0700 hrs. Five hours later, Plt Offs Nash and L A Verrall claimed a Bf 109 fighter-bomber each, and this victory took Peter Nash's tally to 11.5. Scrambled once again soon after returning to Takali, Nash was shot down in BR195 near Dingli when he was bounced by fighters from 6./JG 53.

Five more victories were achieved on the 18th (including one credited to Flt Lt Ron West of No 249 Sqn to make him a Malta ace), although the day's most significant event was the arrival of 17 Spitfires from *Eagle* in Operation *LB*. These were urgently needed, as the fierce fighting of May had taken its toll on Malta's Spitfire force – one Spitfire had been lost and three badly shot up on 18 May alone. The replacement aircraft were the backlog of fighters that had been left behind at Gibraltar due to unserviceability during the recent ferry operations. They had now all been made fully airworthy.

Led in by No 249 Sqn's Flt Lts Lucas and McNair and Flg Off Daddo-Langlois, the remaining 14 pilots included men drawn from UK-based No 130 Sqn, as well as Canadian Jerry Smith, who had been forced to return to *Wasp* with a faulty Slipper tank earlier in the month.

The arrival of these aircraft coincided with the departure of much of II *Fliegerkorps'* fighting strength. It had lost II./JG 3 and II. and III./KG 77 in late April, and now I. and III./JG 53, I./NJG 2, III./ZG 26, III./StG 3 and I./KG 54 left Sicily

Spitfire VC BR195/1-Q was being flown by Plt Off Peter Nash of No 249 Sqn when he scored a shared victory with Plt Off 'Johnny' Plagis (in BR176) over a Bf 109 on 16 May 1942. This success was claimed by the squadron to be its 100th Malta victory. The following day Nash downed another Bf 109 to take his overall score to 11 and 1 shared destroyed, but he was shot down and killed by another Messerschmitt fighter a few hours later (*IWM*)

Plt Off Reade Tilley looks from the cockpit as his groundcrew service his Spitfire VC between sorties at Luqa in late May 1942 (*via Reade Tilley*)

for other fronts. Only II./JG 53, KüFlGr 606 and KGr 806, and air-sea rescue and reconnaissance elements, remained. *Regia Aeronautica* units were transferred in from the Italian mainland to boost numbers.

With the enemy having drastically reduced its force, RAF fighter units on Malta noticed a drop in aerial activity from 19 May through to month-end. Most claims submitted were against Italian fighters and bombers, and one of these (an Re.2001) made Plt Off Reade Tilley an ace on 23 May. Denis Barnham had achieved this distinction two days earlier when had he claimed a Bf 109 and an 'Italian fighter' destroyed.

The series of Spitfire ferry flights in March, April and May, along with the losses inflicted on the Luftwaffe and the *Regia Aeronautica* on the 9th, 10th and 14th of the later month, had really tipped the scales irrevocably in favour of the RAF air defence squadrons. Indeed, there were now so many Spitfires on the island that on 27 May the remaining pilots in No 229 Sqn were sent to other Hurricane units in Egypt and the unit disbanded. It had been sent from North Africa in March to help bolster Malta's defences, and lost six pilots during the fighting. From now on the daytime defence of Malta would be an entirely Spitfire affair.

The victory claims by Spitfire pilots during May had totalled 101 for the loss of 13 pilots killed and 23 fighters destroyed. A handful of aces had been created in all five Spitfire squadrons on Malta, and several had paid the ultimate price.

For the rest of the month, enemy activity was reduced to small numbers of German and Italian bombers escorted by proportionately large numbers of fighters. It was apparent now that if the island were to fall, it would not be by aerial assault. Only if Axis forces could totally blockade the island and starve its inhabitants into submission would Malta wither and die on the vine.

Readiness in Malta

A self-portrait of Flt Lt Denis Barnham at readiness in his Spitfire, showing a combination of concentration, determination, strain and dread. Barnham's book, *One Man's Window*, remains a classic account of the siege of Malta from a fighter pilot's viewpoint. A sensitive and insightful young man, he also was a talented artist who left behind an illustrated diary of his experiences on Malta (*via Frederick Galea*)

DECEPTIVE LULL

June commenced with the launching of Rommel's offensive against Free French forces at Bir Hakeim, in Libya. The British Eighth Army attempted a counterattack, but the rejuvenated *Panzerarmee Afrika* ultimately prevailed and duly set about clearing Libya of Allied forces once and for all. Initially, the German plan was to eradicate the Malta threat, but with the capture of Tobruk (and 35,000 Allied troops and tons of supplies) on 21 June, and what appeared to be the collapse of the Eighth Army, the time now seemed ripe to follow through with a dash across the Egyptian frontier to the Nile Delta. Malta would have to wait.

June would also see the arrival of several fighter pilots on the island who would become aces and high scorers in the coming months. At the same time, the first wave of Spitfire pilots that had flown in during March began to depart for the UK as they became tour-expired.

For much of the month, the Spitfire units were involved in low-intensity operations against Axis intruders, as evidenced by the activity of 1 June. The first day of the month saw just six Bf 109s make a *Jabo* attack in the Tas-Silc area. Eight Spitfires intercepted them, and rising star Flt Sgt 'Slim' Yarra of No 185 Sqn (in GL-K) claimed one shot down and Plt Off Ernie Broad (in BR294/GL-E) damaged a second fighter, but Canadian Plt Off Andy McNaughton was killed (in BP950). This was followed by an unopposed afternoon sweep by C.202s of 155° *Gruppo*.

Ultimately, Yarra would claim 12 fighters destroyed between 12 May and 11 July, with eight of these coming in pairs. His first double haul had been achieved on 15 May when he and Sgt Sim were engaged by seven Bf 109s and four C.202s. Despite the odds, Yarra knocked down two of the Macchis. Three days later he claimed two Bf 109s to achieve ace status, and further doubles came on 21 June (Bf 109s) and 7 July (a C.202 and an Re.2001).

On 3 June another reinforcing flight arrived from *Eagle*. Code-named Operation *Style*, 32 Spitfires were led to Malta by Sqn Ldr Barton, Flt Lt Peck and Flg Off Plagis. Included in this group were future Malta RCAF aces Plt Off Wally McLeod and Flt Sgt James Ballantyne, as well as American Plt Off John Curry, who claimed his first kill over Malta on

These newly repainted Spitfire VCs were photographed at Gibraltar in early June 1942. Shortly thereafter, they were loaded onto *Eagle* and delivered to Malta in Operation *Style*, being led to the island by veteran No 249 Sqn pilots Sqn Ldr Barton, Flt Lt Peck and Flg Off Plagis. This was the ill-fated reinforcement flight that lost four Spitfires shot down by Bf 109s out of 32 that left *Eagle* en route to Malta. This was the only time that the Luftwaffe managed to intercept a Spitfire reinforcement flight, some 13 of which were undertaken between 7 March and 29 October 1942. A total of 396 Spitfires were embarked by four carriers (HMS *Eagle*, *Argus* and *Furious* and USS *Wasp*), of which 367 reached Malta. Twelve aircraft were lost en route to the embattled island (*RAF Museum*)

Flt Lt Henry Wallace McLeod flew into Malta with other reinforcements on 3 June as part of Operation *Style*. He would subsequently run up a score of 13 victories on the island, and later in the war increased his tally to 21 while CO of Spitfire IX-equipped No 443 Sqn RCAF. McLeod was eventually shot down and killed near Nijmegen on 27 September, 1944 when he was bounced by nine Bf 109Gs. He was the highest-scoring RCAF ace of World War 2, although George Beurling was the leading Canadian ace (he scored most of his victories as an RAF pilot) (*via Frederick Galea*)

Spitfire VC BR246 was flown into Malta as part of Operation *Style*. The dark shades of its uppersurface camouflage would suggest that the fighter was painted in Dark Mediterranean Blue, or a mix of similar colours. Quality control was obviously lacking when these desert aircraft were repainted, as BR246 clearly reveals. Missed areas included the serial number, which was often painted over and then crudely reapplied by hand, or not at all. Future RCAF ace Plt Off Frank Jones claimed an Re.2001 from 2° *Gruppo* destroyed while flying this aircraft on the morning of 6 June. He was one of a quartet of No 249 Sqn pilots scrambled at 0920 hrs to intercept 11 Re.2001s that were looking for a missing Italian pilot. The defending Spitfire units claimed to have destroyed no fewer than eight Re.2001s from 2° *Gruppo* on this day (*via Frederick Galea*)

26 June. He subsequently 'made ace' with No 601 Sqn over the Western Desert in October 1942.

All went well with Operation *Style* until, for the first and only time, 12 Bf 109s from II./JG 53 managed to intercept some of the Spitfires as they neared Malta, Two were downed west of Pantelleria and two more near Gozo. A fifth fighter crash-landed at Takali.

6 June brought a renewal of activity, and a disastrous day for 2° *Gruppo*. A dawn patrol by two No 185 Sqn Spitfires downed a Ju 88, and this success was followed up a short while later by a section of No 249 aircraft that claimed two Ju 88s destroyed shortly after 0525 hrs. At 0630 hrs, five Z.1007bis, escorted by 34 C.202s of 155° *Gruppo* and 12 Re.2001s of 2° *Gruppo*, were intercepted by a section of Spitfires from No 249Sqn and 11 fighters from No 603 Sqn. Two Reggiannes was destroyed and several damaged.

At 0920 hrs 11 more Re.2001s were conducting a search for a downed pilot when they were bounced by No 249 Sqn Spitfires. Yet another Italian fighter was lost, and a second one crash-landed in Sicily after being seriously damaged. A second missing pilot search was attempted in the afternoon by six C.202s and 13 Re.2001s, and this resulted in still more losses for 2° *Gruppo*. Among the victors was newly promoted Flt Lt 'Johnny' Plagis (in BR321/GL-J) with two Re.2001s, and future aces Flt Sgt Don 'Shorty' Reid with one Re.2001 and Flt Sgt Wilbert Dodd with a share in the destruction of a Z.506B floatplane. Plagis, who had been made a flight commander with No 185 Sqn on 4 June, later recalled:

'Intercepted about 10–12 enemy aircraft 30–40 miles east of Malta – these were then joined by another 36 enemy aircraft. Reid got one Re.2001. Blue section got the "blood wagon" (Z.506B). I got two Re.2001s destroyed, and both pilots baled out! RIP.'

By the end of the day, the Spitfires had claimed three Ju 88s, one Z.506B and no less than eight Re.2001s of 2° *Gruppo* destroyed.

7 June saw an intrusion by 15 Bf 109s shortly after noon. Eleven Spitfires rose to intercept them, including four from No 185 Sqn. Flt Lt Plagis (again in BR321/GL-J) downed one to bring his Malta tally to ten and two shared destroyed,

Recently promoted Flt Lt 'Johnny' Plagis poses for a photograph in the cockpit of a No 185 Sqn aircraft in late June 1942, by which time he had scored his 11th, and last, Malta victory. His final three kills came with No 185 Sqn, and included two Re.2001s downed on 6 June (*via Dilip Sarkar*)

The conditions on Malta bred improvisation, as seen by this standard Spitfire VC modified to take two 44-gallon Hurricane ferry fuel tanks on a locally made rack. The additional range provided by the fuel in these tanks allowed fighter units to escort the remnants of the vital *Harpoon* convoy into Grand Harbour on 15 June. This field modification was almost certainly unique to Malta-based Spitfires (*via Frederick Galea*)

establishing him as the leading Spitfire ace on the island. He would not claim any further kills prior to being flown to Gibraltar, his tour expired, on 7 July. Upon his arrival in the UK, Plagis was sent to a convalescent home, suffering from malnutrition, scabies and fatigue. Conditions were certainly tough on Malta in 1942.

Two Spitfires were shot down and a pilot killed on 8 June by Bf 109s from II./JG 53, No 603 Sqn losing Plt Off Leslie Barlow (in BR231) and No 249 Sqn having Flt Sgt Butler wounded when he crash-landed BR312 near Takali. No German fighters were downed in return.

These losses were made good on 9 June when a further 32 Spitfires were flown in from *Eagle*, this being the third delivery of fighters to Malta in less than a month. Led in by American ace Plt Off Reade Tilley and New Zealander Flg Off A C Rowe, this group included future aces Plt Off John McElroy RCAF, Plt Off Gray Stenborg RNZAF, Flt Sgt Colin Parkinson RAAF and 20-year-old Canadian (who was a member of the RAF) Sgt George Beurling, who had a reputation for being a loner, as well as a maverick. Beurling would quickly make his mark, rapidly becoming the highest-scoring fighter pilot – Allied or Axis – of the siege. On arrival, Parkinson and McElroy went to No 603 Sqn, Stenborg to No 185 and Beurling to No 249.

During this time, the war was going badly for the Allies in North Africa, with the Eighth Army being being forced to retreat to El Alamein. On Malta, however, the offensive assets were being built up so that an effective campaign could be waged against Rommel's vital Mediterranean supply line. However, food, aviation spirit and AA ammunition remained in short supply on the island. Convoys *Harpoon* (from the west) and *Vigorous* (from the east) were intended to remedy this.

The next major combat took place on 15 June. To cover the incoming convoys (which had been under attack from Axis bombers since 13 June), Spitfires were modified to carry two Hurricane long-range tanks under the centre fuselage. Operating in four-aeroplane sections, the fighters covered *Harpoon*'s approach in relays. First to arrive over the vessels at 1040 hrs were four Spitfires from No 126 Sqn. Although missing Ju 88s in the area, RAAF ace Plt Off Tim Goldsmith downed an RS.14 floatplane that had been shadowing the convoy, and then shared in the destruction of an SM.84 with future ace Flt Sgt Ken Evans (in BR496).

Goldsmith's combat report from the mission read as follows:

'Long-range job. Arrived on convoy 160 miles west of Malta. Found ship burning and sinking. Passed two Italian cruisers on way. Found a three-engined "Dago" floatplane on deck, heading for Pantelleria. Gave him a three-second burst from port cannon and he went in – a flamer. Two 'chutes. On the way home met a C.200 and had a good scrap with him. Left him streaming oil.'

Next to score was No 601 Sqn, adding two Italian-flown Ju 87s to

This Spitfire VC of No 185 Sqn has been painted in the 'standard' Malta air defence colour scheme of Dark Mediterranean Blue, or a mixed equivalent. With the lull in action in mid-June, there was a revision of unit markings. T was adopted by No 249 Sqn, X by No 603 Sqn, MK by No 126 Sqn and GL was applied in yellow to No 185 Sqn's Blue-Grey Spitfires. No 601 Sqn retained its UF codes (*via Frederick Galea*)

BR295 in the foreground was a typical hard-working No 249 Sqn Spitfire. It was used by Kiwi Plt Off Lawrie Verrall to down an Re.2001 from 4° *Stormo* on 27 June. An Operation *Bowery* pilot, Verrall had earlier been credited with a C.202 and a Bf 109 destroyed and a Messerschmitt fighter damaged. Canadian Flt Sgt Bob Middlemiss downed a Bf 109 in BR295 on 2 July, adding this kill to a C.202 destroyed and a Z.1007 shared destroyed over the island (*via Frederick Galea*)

its tally. The unit was then relieved by four No 126 Sqn Spitfires at 1410 hrs. Mixing it over the convoy with Bf 109s, Flt Sgt 'Paddy' Schade (in BP850/F) claimed a Messerschmitt destroyed for his sixth kill:

'Patrolled convoy 140 miles out to sea. Attacked by three Me 109s. Did head-on attack, "Messer" spun down. There was a big splash in the sea. Confident "Messer" went in.'

Next up was No 185 Sqn, whose pilots shot down three Bf 109s and a Ju 88. One of the fighters gave veteran ace Flt Lt Ron West his seventh kill, and Plt Off Gray Stenborg opened his Malta account with another. This was actually Stenborg's fifth victory, for he had downed four Fw 190s over northern France during late April whilst with No 111 Sqn. Later in the day No 601 Sqn downed another Ju 88, and No 249 Sqn added two more Junkers bombers to its scoreboard. The tally for the day was 15 aircraft destroyed (five Ju 88s, four Bf 109s, two Ju 87s, two SM.84s, one Z.506B and one RS.14), but three Spitfires had been lost and New Zealander Sgt Jack McConnell from No 601 Sqn killed.

To date, 213 Spitfires had reached Malta since early March, and with the loss of three aircraft on 15 June, some 55 of these fighters had been shot down. A further 16 had crash-landed due to combat damage, and at least 35 more had been written off on the ground in bombing raids. Finally, 15 machines had been damaged in operational accidents, leaving just 92 serviceable Spitfires split between five units come mid-June.

Despite the best efforts of the Malta Spitfire squadrons, only two of the five merchantmen in the *Harpoon* convoy got through. Worst still, in the eastern Mediterranean *Vigorous* had been forced to turn back in the face of overwhelming Axis air power. This meant that even though Malta's air defence was now at its strongest, essential supplies were beginning to run out and food rations had to be cut yet again.

Skirmishing between the air defence squadrons and Axis fighters took place for the rest of the month, but at a much reduced level. With the easing of pressure on Malta, it was decided that No 601 Sqn could be spared for operations in Egypt. Elements of the unit starting departing the island on 23 June.

During the month of June, the Spitfire squadrons had been credited with 52 victories and 13 probables for the loss of 12 aircraft and two pilots killed. Buoyed by their success against the relief convoys, both the *Regia Aeronautica* and the Luftwaffe now planned to step up the air offensive against Malta.

In support of their Italian allies, the Germans had transferred several highly experienced units from North Africa, France and the Russian front to reinforce II *Fliegerkorps* on Sicily. These included II. and III./KG 77 with Ju 88s and, most ominously, I./JG 77 with Bf 109s. The latter *Gruppe* had a sprinkling of high-scoring aces within its ranks, foremost of whom was *Gruppenkommandeur* Hauptmann Heinz Bär with 113 victories to his credit at that time. The new unit would prove to be a dangerous adversary for the Spitfire squadrons. The month of July would also see the meteoric rise of the greatest Malta ace of them all, George Beurling.

FIGHTER PILOT'S PARADISE

July commenced with the launching of a new Axis offensive directed at Malta's airfields, and Italian units would play a much greater part in this campaign than they had done in recent months. Once again, the island's offensive forces were making inroads into Rommel's supply lines, with the efforts of the No 38 Sqn Wellingtons and Beauforts of Nos 39 and 217 Sqn starting to have an effect on the *Afrika Korps*. The *Regia Aeronautica* initially carried out the brunt of the offensive by itself, but by mid-July it had suffered so many losses that German units were forced to take over. Indeed, this month would see the Spitfire units on Malta making the second highest number of victory claims of the entire siege.

The new offensive kicked off during the afternoon of 1 July with the approach of a single Ju 88, escorted by C.202s from 20° *Gruppo* and Bf 109s from 5./JG 53. No 185 Sqn's 'B' Flight intercepted the force, and Flight Leader Plt Off Hal Halford claimed a Bf 109 destroyed, as did future RCAF ace Flt Sgt Don Reid (in BR294/GL-E). 'Slim' Yarra wrote:

'F/Sgt Reid destroyed a Me 109 and damaged another. This brings "Shorty's" score to four destroyed, which is a very good performance on the part of the "Kid".'

Seated in his personally marked Spitfire (BR387/GL-W), Australian ace Plt Off John 'Slim' Yarra accounted for 12 enemy aircraft over Malta. He downed two Bf 109s, two Re.2001s and a Ju 88 with BR387, which he christened *NED* after his girlfriend Doreen (she was nicknamed 'Ned'). All of his Spitfires bore the same name, with BR387 being *NED IV*. Yarra flew this aircraft over Malta for the last time on 16 July 1942 (*via Frederick Galea*)

EP200/GL-T was one of the most photographed fighters on the island. Arriving on 21 July 1942, this Spitfire VB of No 185 Sqn was flown by Australian 8.333-victory ace Flt Lt Colin Parkinson, amongst others, until it was finally lost to Axis flak over Sicily on 27 August whilst being flown by American Flg Off P A Woodger, who became a PoW. Several photographs were also taken of it crashed on Sicily (*via Frederick Galea*)

Shown from another angle, freshly repainted EP200/GL-T was almost certainly camouflaged in Light Mediterranean Blue or Extra Dark Sea Grey, leaving large areas of Dark Earth intact. Unusually, the individual code letter T was painted white, while the unit codes were almost certainly applied in No 185 Sqn's standard yellow (*via Frederick Galea*)

This opening attack was followed by an even larger raid at 1845 hrs when two SM.84s and 22 C.202s approached the island, followed by a second wave consisting of three SM.84s escorted by 48 C.202s from 51° *Gruppo* and 15 Re.2001s from 2° *Gruppo*. They were engaged by 12 Spitfires from No 603 Sqn, and Flt Sgt Jimmy Ballantyne (flying BR367/X-O) scored his first kill when he downed a 'Bf 109' and claimed a second one damaged. He was then forced to bale out after his aircraft was shot up, Ballantyne being plucked from the water by rescue launch HSL 107. Another rising star to score his first victory (an Re.2001) in this engagement was Australian Flt Sgt Colin Parkinson in BR184/X-C.

The next day, eight No 185 Sqn Spitfires were scrambled, followed by eight from No 603 Sqn, when 18 Bf 109s were detected off the coast. Four headed inland, one of which was shot down by Flt Sgt 'Shorty' Reid (in BR294/GL-E) for his fifth victory. Sadly, ace Plt Off Johnny Hurst (in BR184) from Kent failed to return – he had been the first pilot from No 603 Sqn to be decorated on the island. American Plt Off Harry Kelly (in BR184/C) of No 249 Sqn was also killed, while No 185 Sqn's Plt Off N J 'Buzz' Ogilvie RCAF crash-landed in what was becoming an ace Spitfire, BR387/GL-W, which was the usual mount of 'Slim' Yarra.

Two more major raids were flown that day, as well as a minor one. A pattern was now developing that saw three raids being sent against Malta per day – one in the morning, one around noon and one in the late afternoon/evening, sometimes supplemented by a night raid.

BR295 of No 249 Sqn is seen here in the company of BR130/T-D at Takali in July 1942 (*IWM*)

On 6 July there were no fewer than six incursions into Maltese airspace. This was the first day in which the air fighting prowess of Sgt George Beurling manifested itself. Enemy activity started with an early morning raid headed for Takali, consisting of six Ju 88s escorted by 15–20 Bf 109s. No 603 Sqn attempted to intercept the German aircraft, but little contact was made. For their efforts, the enemy damaged a solitary Spitfire in its pen at the base.

Hot on the heels of this raid came an even larger one consisting of three Z.1007bis from 9° *Stormo*, with 14 Re.2001s from 2° *Gruppo* and 24 C.202s from 20° *Gruppo* offering indirect support. Even more C.202s from 151ª *Squadrigilia*, led by seven-kill ace Capitano Furio Doglio Niclot, swept in ahead of this armada. Flt Lt Norman Lee (in BR379/T-V) led ten No 249 Sqn Spitfires in a head-on attack on the bombers, and four pilots gained strikes, including Sgt Beurling (in BR323/T-S). He then scored his first Malta kill by shooting down a C.202 from 20° *Gruppo* flown by Sergente Francesco Pecchiari of 352ª *Squadrigilia*, which was quickly followed by another claim for a Macchi. This was probably an Re.2001 of 152ª *Squadrigilia*, as described by Beurling:

'As the bombers turned to run in, I saw a Macchi 202 boring up "Smitty's" [Flg Off John Smith] tail. I did a quick climbing turn and bored in on the "Eyetie", catching him unawares. A one-second burst smacked him in the engine and glycol tank. He burst into flames and went down like a plummet. The same performance followed with another Macchi. Like the first one, this baby picked on "Smitty", and I on "Smitty's" friend. He saw me coming, however, and I broke away by diving for the ground. We went down vertically together from 20,000 ft to about 5000 ft, and I let him have it from about 300 yards and slightly to starboard as he pulled out. God knows where I hit him, but he exploded into a million pieces. Number two.'

Later that morning another raid (this time by five Ju 88s and 15 to 20 Bf 109s) was intercepted by 27 Spitfires from Nos 185 and 603 Sqns. Three Ju 88s and two Bf 109s

BR130 was coded T-D, as confirmed by photographs such as this one and the shot on page 55, but it was marked up as 2-H when flown off *Wasp* on 20 April 1942. And by October its codes had apparently been changed to T-S. By November 1943 the fighter had been passed on to the USAAF. In the background is Spitfire VB EN976/T-C, which was flown at various times by Canadian aces Plt Offs John 'Willie the Kid' Williams and John McElroy (*IWM*)

Malta's ace of aces, Plt Off George Beurling, adds the finishing touches to his scoreboard. This photograph was almost certainly taken after the ranking Canadian ace had left Malta and returned to the UK to fly Spitfire IXs with the RCAF. Note the well worn appearance of his peaked cap! (*via Bruce Robertson*)

were downed by the defenders, with RCAF ace Flt Sgt Wilbert Dodd getting both Messerschmitts to take his tally to four and one shared.

At 1840 hrs, yet another raid approached comprised of four Z.1007bis and 39 C.202s, and this was countered by 17 Spitfires from Nos 126 and 603 Sqns. Keeping the pressure on the defenders, the fifth raid of a very hectic and intense day came at 2030 hrs when three Ju 88s from II./KG 77, escorted by two-dozen Bf 109s from II./JG 53 and I./JG 77, came in at low level to bomb Takali. Two of the bombers were shot down and victory claims were submitted for three Bf 109s.

'B' Flight of No 249 Sqn pose for a photograph in early July 1942. Third from left is highly regarded Sqn Ldr 'Laddie' Lucas and holding the bomb is leading Malta ace Sgt George Beurling. Lucas left the island shortly after this photograph was taken by flight commander Flt Lt Norman Lee (*via Patrick Lee*)

'Screwball' Beurling entered the ranks of the aces by turning the tables on two Messerschmitts that had bounced him. Doing a quick wingover, he got on the tail of one of his opponents, which then tried to climb away. At a range of about 800 yards, Beurling let fly with a three-second burst at full deflection. Streaming white smoke, the fighter went down in flames and hit the water. His victim was most likely Felwebel Anton Engels of I./JG 77. Having claimed two Fw 190s over France with No 41 Sqn in early May, Beurling's trio of victories on 6 July now took his tally to five.

The 7th was yet another day of high-intensity combat, with an early morning raid by 12 Ju 88s on Luqa. The bombers were escorted by 24 Bf 109s from II./JG 53 and 30 C.202s from 20° *Gruppo* and 155° *Gruppo*. At 0730 hrs, 12 No 249 Sqn Spitfires, followed by six more from No 185 Sqn, were scrambled. Australian veteran Plt Off Paul Brennan was leading four aircraft in No 249 Sqn's 'Green' section up to 20,000 ft when he spotted six Ju 88s below him flying in line abreast formartion. Diving on the bombers, Brennan soon found himself being pursued by three Bf 109s. As soon as he had gathered speed, he whipped AB526 out of their line of fire, skidded to the left as a Bf 109 sped by and then locked onto its tail. The ace delivered a three-second burst, hitting the engine. The fighter fell away in a spiral dive and crashed into the sea. Brennan, on his last Malta mission, had scored his tenth, and final, victory of the war.

Also involved in this action was newcomer Canadian Plt Off John McElroy, who downed a Bf 109 for his first victory over Malta – he was flying BR301/UF-S, which was an ex-No 601 Sqn aircraft. In all, three Bf 109s and a C.202 were claimed against the loss of two Spitfires, although the pilots were rescued. A midday sweep by 19 Bf 109s cost the air defence units two more Spitfires shot down (killing both No 185 Sqn pilots) and two more crash-landed. These losses were balanced against claims for five Bf 109s destroyed, two of which were credited to 'Paddy' Schade of No 126 Sqn, raising his score to ten and one shared.

The last raid of the day consisted of five Z.1007bis with an escort of 35 C.202s and 12 Re.2001s. They were met by 22 Spitfires from Nos 185 and 603 Sqns, and Flt Sgt 'Slim' Yarra brought down two Re.2001s to

Spitfire VC MK-N of No 126 Sqn was camouflaged in a very dark uppersurface colour thought to be Dark Mediterranean Blue, with Sky Blue undersides. Numerous pilots flew this aircraft, including leading squadron ace Flt Sgt Paddy Schade. He claimed two Bf 109s destroyed in MK-N on 9 July 1942, and finished his tour on Malta with a tally of 13.5 kills (*via Frederick Galea*)

take his score to 11, thus equalling 'Johnny' Plagis' tally.

The pattern of a morning, noon and late afternoon raid by the Luftwaffe and *Regia Aeronautica* continued for the next few days. On 8 July, Sgt Beurling claimed a Bf 109 shot down and future Canadian ace Plt Off John 'Willie the Kid' Williams of No 249 Sqn opened his Malta account with a Bf 109 and a Ju 88 destroyed. Kiwi Plt Off Ray Hesselyn marked his last operational sortie over Malta by knocking down two Bf 109s in BR562, thus making him the island's leading ace again with 12 victories. He would not top the list for long, however.

The very next day Flt Sgt 'Paddy' Schade was credited with two Bf 109s destroyed, making him the new top scorer on the island with 12.5 victories. His brace came whilst opposing an evening raid on Takali by six Ju 88s, which were escorted by a large number of Bf 109s from II./JG 53 and I./JG 77. Some 35 Spitfires from Nos 126, 185, 249 and 603 Sqns opposed the German formation. Schade's combat report stated:

'Attacked two Me 109s off Filfla. Fired three-second burst at port Messerschmitt. Strikes along fuselage. White smoke issued and it hit the sea. Attacked two more Messerschmitts northwest of Gozo. Strikes were seen along starboard wing. White smoke poured out from the enemy aircraft. Two Me 109s destroyed.'

Schade still a few more days to go before he was declared tour-expired, but Hesselyn's time on Malta was now over. Posted back to England as an instructor, he would pass on his knowledge of air fighting to new pilots until he returned to operational flying on the Channel front in June 1943. Hesselyn duly claimed an additional 6.5 kills before being shot down over France four months later. He spent the rest of the war as a PoW.

Although a considerable number of victories had been scored on 8 and 9 July, these had come at some cost to the defenders, for five Spitfire pilots had been killed in action. Three more would perish in the next 72 hours.

New Zealander Plt Off Gray Stenborg of No 185 Sqn had matched Flt Sgt Schade's brace of Bf 109s on the 9th (in Spitfire BR109), thus giving him five Malta victories, and nine overall.

Despite the *Regia Aeronautica* and the Luftwaffe having suffered numerous casualties, the Axis offensive continued, although it was now beginning to lose momentum. Badly mauled and totally demoralised, the Italian bomber force had ceased flying sorties over Malta by the end of the first week in July. All bombing missions were now being conducted by the Ju 88s units. Serviceability problems were also affecting the sortie rate of the C.202 units. Increasingly, the Luftwaffe was having to play a greater role in the raids. This mattered very little to Sgt Beurling, however, as he was happy to shoot down Germans and Italians alike – indeed, on 10 July he had become a true Malta ace when he destroyed both a C.202 and a Bf 109 (in BR323/S).

Canadian Plt Off John 'Willie the Kid' Williams had flown into Malta with Operation *Bowery* on 9 May 1942. Posted to No 249 Sqn, he became a close friend of Sgt George Beurling, and was frequently mentioned in the ace's book *Malta Spitfire*, published in 1943. After a slow start in May and June (during which time he claimed five Axis aircraft damaged in combat), Williams scored four victories in July and two during the October *Blitz*. Completing his tour on 31 October, he boarded a No 511 Sqn Liberator heading back to the UK that same evening, along with 23 other tour-expired or wounded pilots (including Plt Off Beurling) and ten civilians. The aircraft subsequently overshot the runway at Gibraltar due to poor weather conditions and crashed into the sea. Sadly, Williams was amongst the 14 passengers who did not survive the accident (*via Frederick Galea*)

The 11th July began with yet another raid on Takali at 0925 hrs by 18 Ju 88s, escorted by 23 C.202s and 24 Bf 109s. The Axis fighters successfully warded off most of the attacks by No 249 Sqn, although the unit claimed two Messerschmitts destroyed. There followed a lull until 1430 hrs, when ten Ju 88s, escorted by Re.2001s and Bf 109s, arrived over the island and were countered by eight Spitfires from No 126 Sqn. The latter unit was duly credited with downing a bomber and an Italian fighter.

The last raid of the day again targeted Takali, with ten Ju 88s, escorted by 24 Bf 109s and 16 C.202s, being opposed by 24 Spitfires (eight each from Nos 126, 249 and 185 Sqns). In the ensuing combats, each of the RAF units claimed a Bf 109 destroyed, with the No 126 Sqn kill being made by Flt Sgt 'Paddy' Schade during his second scramble on the 11th. He had been attacked by two fighters, one of which, in his words, 'jumped me, but it went straight into the drink. I didn't fire my guns at all! One Me 109 destroyed.' This was his sixth victory in a week, and his last over Malta, taking his tally to 13.5 overall.

Also scoring the last victory of his Malta tour was No 185 Sqn's Plt Off 'Slim' Yarra (in BR305/GL-N), whose tally now stood at 12:

'Scrambled after 40+ plot. Joined up with another Spit. Saw two '109s and attacked one and shot it down (yellow-nosed). The other boys could not get amongst the Jerries so we had to be content with one victory for the day. Escorted shot-up Spit back to base.'

Yarra was the leading Australian ace of the Malta campaign, who flew for the last time over the island on 16 July in his personally marked Spitfire VC BR387/GL-W. Upon returning to the UK, Yarra was posted to No 453 Sqn RAAF as a flight commander, and on 10 December 1942 he was killed when shot down by a flak ship during an attack on a German convoy off the Dutch coast. His brother, who was also a fighter pilot, was subsequently killed in combat as well.

On 12 July the Axis attacks followed the usual pattern of morning, noon and afternoon raids of ten or so Ju 88s, escorted by large numbers of fighters. The defenders claimed six aircraft destroyed, with three of these being credited to Beurling. During his second sortie of the day, the Canadian ace (in BR565/T-T) downed two Re.2001s that were searching for Reggiane pilot Tenente Francesco Vichi – Beurling had shot the pilot down during the noon raid. Covered by Flg Off E L Hetherington, Beurling bounced the Italian fighters, despatching the aircraft flown by Tenente Carlo Seganti from close range. He then closed in on the second Re.2001, piloted by Tenente Colonello Aldo Quarantotti:

'I closed up to 30 yards, and I was on his port side coming in at an angle of about 15 degrees. I could see all the details in his face because he turned around and looked at me just as I had a bead on him.'

Beurling fired a short burst that decapitated the pilot. His body, still strapped into the seat of his aircraft, spewed blood from the stump of his neck, which streamed down the side of the fuselage. Despite Beurling's well-known public bravado, it is said that this incident haunted him for the rest of his short life.

Three more raids on Maltese airfields kept the Spitfire units busy on 13 July, with the first of these targeting Luqa. At 0800 hrs, 18 Ju 88s, escorted by 24 Bf 109s, ten C.202s and six Re.2001s, were intercepted by Nos 185, 603 and 126 Sqns. Future aces Sgt Arthur Varey and Flt Sgt

The changing of the Guard. On 15 July, AVM Keith Park (right) arrived on Malta to take over command of Malta's air defence from AVM Hugh Lloyd, who was now tour-expired. Lloyd was a former bomber pilot who had been brought in to build up Malta's offensive capacity, and had seen it through the worst days of the siege. However, it was felt by some of the more senior fighter pilots on the island that he never really understood how best to use the Hurricane and Spitfire squadrons at his disposal, or understood their operational requirements. AVM Keith Park, who had commanded No 11 Group during the Battle of Britain, was very much a fighter pilot's advocate. He soon implemented the Fighter Interception Plan, which called for the forward interception of raids to the north of the island before the bombers hit their targets (*IWM*)

Canadian pilot Flt Sgt Ian Maclennan initially served with No 610 Sqn before moving to No 401 Sqn RCAF in April 1942. Whilst with the latter unit he collided with another Spitfire whilst taking off – 'we met and kissed in the middle', he later recalled. This was Maclennan's second accident in only a matter of weeks, and after being reprimanded by his CO, future USAAF ace Sqn Ldr Don Blakeslee, it was decided that the best place for him was Malta. He flew off *Eagle* on 9 June 1942 as part of Operation *Salient* and was held in the pilot pool on the island until posted to No 1435 Flt on 21 July. Scoring two kills in August, Maclennan followed this up with four victories in the October *Blitz* and a final success on 14 November. He was posted back to the UK the following month, returning to operations in February 1944 with Spitfire IX-equipped No 443 Sqn RCAF. Maclennan was shot down by flak near the Normandy beachhead on 7 June, becoming a PoW and ending up at Stalag Luft III at Sagan not long after the 'Great Escape'. There, he was employed by the escape committee as a mapmaker. After breaking away from a column being marched toward the Danube in the closing weeks of the war, Maclennan eventually reached Allied lines (*via Frederick Galea*)

Ken Evans downed a Ju 88 and C.202 respectively, while Plt Off John McElroy of No 249 Sqn (in BR301/UF-S) got a Bf 109. The noon raid by seven Ju 88s slipped in unopposed, followed by the usual late afternoon attack.

At this point the Italian offensive faltered and lost momentum as virtually all *Regia Aeronautica* units were replaced by German ones. On the 14th just one raid targeted Malta, and for the next nine days far fewer Axis bombers were seen over the island.

CHANGE OF COMMAND

This slowing in the operational tempo coincided with the the arrival of AVM Keith Park, who flew to Malta aboard a Sunderland on the 14th to relieve the tour-expired AVM Lloyd. Park brought with him the highly experienced Wg Cdr John M Thompson, who had claimed six kills flying Hurricane Is with No 111 Sqn in 1940. He had been a proponent of head-on attacks on bomber formations in the Battle of Britain, and had been picked by Park to impart his knowledge to the air defence units.

Park, a 20-victory ace in World War 1, and a true fighter pilot's man, had led No 11 Group in the Battle of Britain. His group had borne the brunt of the Luftwaffe assault in 1940, and his leadership of it was considered to be one of the key elements in winning the battle.

Park's predecessor on Malta, AVM Lloyd, had directed his squadrons through the darkest days of the siege, and had never failed to maintain the air defence of the island, or attack enemy supply lines when possible. However, being an ex-bomber pilot it was felt by the air defence pilots that he never really grasped the dynamics and tactics of fighter combat. Nevertheless, he had seen the defence of the island through the worst of times, and was honoured and revered by the people of Malta.

Park immediately put into operation his Fighter Interception Plan. From now on, the interception of raids would take place north of Malta before the bombers reached their targets. The plan called for a response by three units – one to take on the high cover, one to deal with the close escort and one to make a head-on attack on the bombers. A fourth unit, if available, would deal with any bombers that managed to break through.

Despite the successes of the last two weeks, no fewer than 39 Spitfires had been lost, damaged or written off in accidents between 1 and 15 July. This figure represented about 40 per cent of the day fighter force. Another reinforcement of Spitfires was urgently needed, and 31 fighters were flown off *Eagle* on the 15th in Operation *Pinpoint* – the 32nd aircraft (EP117) hit the ship's bridge on take-off and had to be pushed over the side. The remaining Spitfires made it safely to Malta. Reinforcement continued the next day when HMS *Welshman* made a high-speed run to the island with badly needed supplies.

This time the Spitfires brought in were tropicalised Mk VBs instead of VCs, which had been the staple type since April. Included in this draft of pilots were future RCAF aces Plt Off Rod Smith and Flt Sgt Ian Maclennan, and 19-year-old American Claude Weaver III, who was the son of a prominent Oklahoma politician. Smith would go to No 126 Sqn and join his brother Jerry, Maclennan to the newly formed No 1435 Flt and Weaver to No 185 Sqn.

Sporadic raiding continued, but not with the intensity of earlier in the month. Another fly off occurred on the 21st from *Eagle*, code-named Operation *Insect*. Again, 32 Spitfire VBs trops were sent, but one crashed soon after take-off and a second was damaged on the deck of the carrier. The remaining 30 made it safely to Malta. Yet another future ace in the form of Plt Off William 'Wally' Walton flew in with these aircraft and was sent to No 1435 Flt. This unit had actually reformed as a Day Fighter Flight at Luqa on the very day Walton reached Malta.

Under the command of ace Sqn Ldr Tony Lovell, and with flight commanders Flt Lts John Halford and Wally McLeod, No 1435 Flt had previously been the island's Night Fighter Flight, equipped with Hurricanes. It was initially issued with surplus Spitfires and eventually acquired full squadron status on 2 August with the arrival of new pilots.

Despite a scaling down of the Axis offensive, action continued through to the end of July, and a further seven Spitfire pilots were killed. Amongst them were five-victory RCAF ace Plt Off D G 'Shorty' Reid of No 185 Sqn and French-Canadian Plt Off Jean Paradis of No 249 Sqn, both of whom perished in the same action fighting Bf 109s from I./JG 77 on the 22nd. Reid and Paradis (who was a friend of George Beurling) were part of a 14-aircraft formation that had intercepted an incoming raid of Ju 88s and Bf 109s off Zonqor Point. Paradis, flying BR128/3-W, was last heard saying 'I see bombair – I go dere.' Reid saw Paradis go in, went to investigate and was last seen engaging a Bf 109 in BR203/X.

The Luftwaffe persisted with its bombing campaign, and on 25 July Park's Fighter Interception Plan was implemented. Previously, due to the small number of defending fighters on Malta, units would fly south of the

Plt Off Rod Smith, younger brother of Plt Off Jerry Smith, who landed his Spitfire on *Wasp*, joined him in No 126 Sqn after arriving on Malta on 15 July 1942 as part of Operation *Pinpoint*. He would claim 6.25 kills whilst flying from the island, and survived the war with a score of 13.25 victories (*via Norman Franks*)

No 185 Sqn's Plt Off Don 'Shorty' Reid was only 5 ft 4.5 in tall, making him one of the shortest aviators in the RCAF. A *Bowery* reinforcement pilot, he was certainly in the thick of the fighting in June and July 1942. He scored five victories in seven weeks, including two in BR294/GL-E on 1 July. He was shot down and killed by Bf 109s from I./JG 77 on 22 July in BR203/X (*via Frederick Galea*)

island to gain height, before attacking any enemy aircraft that presented themselves. The strategy now was to meet the enemy bombers north of the island before they reached their targets.

On the 26th, the intensity of enemy bombing raids increased once again, but Malta was now striking back. Park's desire for a more offensive posture manifested itself that night when three Hurricanes armed with 250-lb bombs attempted to bomb Gela airfield. One of the participants was Sgt Claude Weaver, who had already claimed 5.5 kills since his arrival on 15 July. Only one Hurricane actually bombed the airfield, but this was just a forerunner of things to come.

The 27th proved to be the most hectic day of combat since 14 July, and it witnessed one of Sgt Beurling's most famous combats. At 0830 hrs, nine Ju 88s, with an escort of Bf 109s and 13 C.202s, headed for Takali. The Macchis were engaged by six Spitfires from No 249 Sqn, with Sgt Beurling (in BR301/UF-S) moving in on four fighters that were flying in line astern formation. As they pulled into a climbing turn to the right, Beurling fired a burst at the fourth C.202. He later recalled:

'It was a straight deflection shot that went into his engine and radiator. He flicked into a spin but managed to pull out, crash-landing on Gozo. He was able to walk away from the mess.'

The pilot, Sergente Falerio Gelli, subsequently became famous for being possibly the only airman to survive being shot down by Beurling. The Canadian immediately fired at another C.202, which, as he put it, 'simply blew into pieces in the air'. This turned out to be the aircraft of Italy's leading Malta ace (with seven victories), Capitano Furio Doglio Niclot, commander of 151ª *Squadriglia*. He died instantly. Spotting two Bf 109s below him, Beurling immediately gave chase:

'I half-rolled and shot past the Messerschmitts, pulling up sharply under their bellies. I let the first guy have it full-out and caught him in the gas tank. Down he went.'

He then damaged the other, which beat a hasty retreat to Sicily minus bits of its wings. Other pilots were busy in this swirling air battle too, and three more Bf 109s were claimed destroyed. One of these fell to future ace Plt Off 'Willie the Kid' Williams of No 249 Sqn in EN976/T-C.

A lunchtime raid by five Ju 88s and Bf 109 escorts was countered by 25 Spitfires drawn from Nos 126, 185, 249 and 603 Sqns. The seven fighters from No 126 Sqn met the bombers in a line abreast attack, while six No 249 Sqn Spitfires dealt with the escort. Plt Off Williams got his second victory of the day in EN976/T-C and Sgt Beurling destroyed yet another Bf 109 in BR301/UF-S. This kill brought the Canadian's Malta score to 14, making him the leading ace of the campaign – a position he would occupy for the remainder of the siege, and beyond.

This aircraft was amongst the first Spitfire VBs that started to arrive on Malta in July. Its blue-grey camouflage scheme faded dramatically after only a few weeks in the Mediterranean sun (*IWM*)

Between 6 and 29 July, 20-year-old Sgt George Beurling had claimed 15 kills – six Bf 109s, five C.202s and four Re.2001s. He had achieved three victories twice during this period (on the 6th and the 12th), and four on the 27th. Including his two Fw 190s from May, Beurling's overall tally now stood at 17 kills and 7 damaged.

Another raid followed at 2000 hrs on the 27th, with the usual combination of Ju 88s, Bf 109s and C.202s. The defenders claimed two C.202s, four Ju 88s and no less than nine Bf 109s destroyed. Two hours later the Hurricane intruders were out again, targeting Comiso, on Sicily. Led by veteran Hurricane pilot Wg Cdr Stan Turner, Sgts Claude Weaver and Len Reid succeeded in hitting the airfield.

More victories and more losses (including two pilots killed from No 1435 Flt) came during the final four days of July, with the Spitfire units continuing to tangle with Bf 109s in the main – few Italian aircraft were now being encountered.

Virtually from start to finish, July had been a month of intense combat. Spitfire pilots had flown 1780 sorties and claimed 142 aircraft destroyed (a figure only surpassed by the victory tally for October 1942, which would total 144.5) for the loss of 38 Spitfires. The tonnage of bombs dropped had dramatically tailed away in the second half of the month (160 tons versus 389 tons), due in no small part to AVM Park's new tactics causing an unacceptably high attrition rate amongst the Ju 88s – at least 22 had been lost, along with a dozen Z.1007 and SM.84 bombers.

The air defence of Malta had turned the corner, and there was definitely no looking back. Despite the successes of this month, however, a chronic shortage of food, fuel and, to a lesser extent, AA ammunition, remained the island's greatest problem due to the ongoing Axis blockade of the central Mediterranean. Starvation loomed in the immediate future unless drastic measures were taken.

This is thought to be the only photograph in existence of the highest-scoring Spitfire of the Malta siege, Mk VC BR301/UF-S of No 249 Sqn. Its serial can be partially seen on the aircraft's tail section. BR301 was flown by Plt Off John McElroy RCAF (2.5/0/1), Flt Sgt Mickey Butler RCAF (0/0/1), Plt Off Alan Yates RAAF (0.5/0/0), Sgt George Beurling (5/0/2), Plt Off Jack Rae RNZAF (0/1.5/2), Plt Off John Williams RCAF (0/0/1) and Sqn Ldr Richard Mitchell (1/0/0) in July 1942. Its total number of victories came to eight and two shared destroyed, one and one shared probables and seven damaged (*IWM*)

PEDESTAL CONVOY AND OCTOBER BLITZ

Although the defenders of Malta now had the upper hand in the air battle for the island, the 'noose' in the form of the Axis blockade was tightening, and Allied forces would be forced to surrender or starve if nothing less than a big convoy failed to get through in August. And although the situation on the ground in North Africa had not improved for the Allies as the summer wore on, the fall of the garrison at Tobruk now meant that Middle East Command could focus its undivided attention on resupplying Malta.

The *Afrika Korps*' stunning advance eastward into Egypt also played into Malta's hands, as the Axis supply chain was now at its most stretched. Rommel desperately needed troops and equipment as he prepared for the pivotal Battle of El Alamein, and it would be up to Malta's offensive assets to hinder the flow of food, fuel, ammunition and reinforcements to the *Afrika Korps* – much to the consternation of Germany's High Command.

August began with a greatly reduced level of air activity, which came as a relief to the defenders of Malta following the ferocious air battles that were fought on a near daily basis throughout July. On the 2nd, four Ju 88s and their fighter escort approached the island, but of the 23 Spitfires that were scrambled to intercept them, just eight from No 185 Sqn made contact and only Sgt Claude Weaver (in EP139) was able to claim a probable Bf 109 kill. Two Spitfires were lost to the Bf 109s, however, with Plt Off J W Guthrie and Kiwi Sgt M L McLeod losing their lives.

The following day a new Spitfire unit was created at Takali in the form of No 229 Sqn – No 1435 Flt had been given squadron status 24 hours earlier. Initially, these units were provided with pilots and aircraft previously assigned to No 603 Sqn, but on 11 August 37 additional Spitfires flew in from HMS *Furious* in Operation *Bellows*.

On 7 August the Luqa Spitfire Wing welcomed new CO Wg Cdr Peter Prosser Hanks, who already had nine victories to his name when he arrived on Malta. He would claim another four victories during the fighting in October, and later lead the Hal Far Wing too.

Three days later, Ju 88s, escorted by Bf 109s from II./JG 53, headed for Malta for the first time that month. The raiders, targeting Luqa, were intercepted by Nos 126 and 1435 Sqns. The latter unit claimed three fighters destroyed, one of which was downed by Flt Lt Wally McLeod (his fourth kill) and another by future ace Flt Sgt Ian Maclennan (his first kill). Later that day, two Spitfires from No 126 Sqn that were on patrol over minesweepers went after a lone Ju 88, and only one of them returned. The missing pilot was Plt Off Jerry Smith, who famously made the first

Flt Lt W J Johnson flew into Malta from *Eagle* on 9 May 1942 during Operation *Bowery*. A veteran of previous combat tours with Nos 85, 145 and 611 Sqns on the Channel Front, he had a single kill to his credit when he joined No 126 Sqn. Johnson became temporary CO of the unit from 27 July after its CO, Sqn Ldr Phil Winfield, was seriously wounded. Following a slow start, Johnson subsequently ran up a score of 5.58 victories over Malta, including two C.202s destroyed (in BR311/L-MK) on 14 August whilst defending the vessels of Operation *Pedestal* from aerial attack (*via Frederick Galea*)

Spitfire landing on a carrier. His brother Rod helped search the sea for him but no trace of the pilot was ever found. Jerry Smith had claimed three confirmed, one and one shared probables and four damaged prior to his death (in BR366).

That same day (10 August), a new convoy, code-named Operation *Pedestal*, set sail for Malta from Gibraltar. The nucleus of the convoy – 13 fast freighters and the US-owned Texaco oil tanker *Ohio* – had assembled in the River Clyde in late July, where they were loaded with 85,000 tons of urgently needed supplies. The merchantmen had picked up their escorts in Gibraltar, Force 'F' consisting of no less than two battleships, seven light cruisers, 26 destroyers and three aircraft carriers (HMS *Victorious*, HMS *Indomitable* and HMS *Eagle*), whose fighters would provide air cover.

The epic voyage of the *Pedestal* convoy is outside the scope of this narrative, but the eventual arrival of the surviving merchantmen and *Ohio* in Grand Harbour on 15 August ensured that the Allies would stave off defeat yet again. But this survival came at a very high cost, for nine freighters were sunk and 300 seamen killed. A number of warships were sunk too, including *Eagle*, which had ferried Spitfires to Malta on ten occasions in 1942. *Furious* would be the sole carrier used for further reinforcement flights, and it delivered another batch on 17 August – 29 of the 32 Spitfires involved in Operation *Baritone* made it safely to Malta.

This latest draft of pilots allowed the release of several tour–expired aircrew, including eight-victory American ace Plt Off Reade Tilley, who had been on the island since late April.

On 18 August another American pilot continued his run of victories. Sgt Claude Weaver of No 185 Sqn was part of a four-aeroplane section led by Plt Off Gray Stenborg that encountered six Bf 109s over Kalafrana. Weaver (in BR374) claimed two destroyed and Stenborg (in EP457) got a third. However, the latter pilot's aircraft had sustained damage of its own and he was forced to bale out over water. Stenborg was soon rescued.

On 27 August there was more excitement, as Spitfires carried out a rare daylight strike on Sicilian airfields. At 1300 hrs, ten No 185 Sqn Spitfires led by Wg Cdr J M Thompson and Maj C J O Swales headed for Comiso. They were followed in five-minute intervals by eight Spitfires from No 229 Sqn, led by Gp Capt W M Churchill (station commander at Takali) and Wg Cdr A H Donaldson (Wing Commander Flying at Takali), which headed for Biscari. Eight more fighters from No 249 Sqn, led by unit CO Sqn Ldr E N Woods, targeted Gela.

No 185 Sqn came across eight Ju 88s near Comiso and claimed

Native Oklahoman Claude Weaver dropped out of high school in February 1941 to join the RCAF. Once in the UK, he was assigned to No 412 Sqn RCAF. However, within three months he was headed to Malta, flying a Spitfire VB off *Eagle* on 15 July 1942. Posted to No 185 Sqn at Hal Far, Weaver began scoring immediately. He shot down a Bf 109 (in BR292) on the 17th, followed by two Bf 109s on the 22nd and two more on the 23rd (all four in EP122). Weaver then claimed a share in a Ju 88 on the 24th. During the latter part of the month he flew night intruder sorties over Sicily in a bomb-carrying Hurricane. On 31 July he was shot up by ace Oberleutnant Gerhard Michalski of II./JG 53 and forced to crash-land in EP343. By the time Weaver force-landed on Sicily during yet another sweep of the island on 9 September, his score had increased to ten and one shared destroyed. A year after being made a PoW, he was able to escape at the time of the Italian Armistice and make his way to Allied lines. Posted back to the UK, Weaver was sent to No 403 Sqn RCAF. He scored two more victories prior to being shot down and killed during a 'Ranger' over northern France on 28 January 1944 (*via Frederick Galea*)

Wg Cdr J M Thompson had joined the RAF in 1934, and had been in the thick of the action over France and southern England in 1940 whilst serving with No 111 Sqn. An early advocate of head-on attacks on German bomber formations during this time, he had claimed six kills in 1940. Accompanying Malta's new AOC, AVM Keith Park, to the island in July 1942, Thompson initially took over the Takali Wing, but was then moved to Hal Far with the arrival of Wg Cdr Arthur Donaldson. He added two more victories to his tally during the 'October *Blitz*'. At the end of 1942 Thompson took over the Luqa Wing, and thus became the only pilot to lead all three Malta air defence wings (*via Frederick Galea*)

four of them shot down – one fell to Sgt Weaver, who also claimed a Bf 109 that was trying to take off and intercept the intruders. These successes were tempered by the death of Gp Capt Walter Churchill (who had claimed four and three shared victories with No 3 Sqn in France in 1940), who was hit by flak. American Flg Off P A Woodger of No 185 Sqn also crash-landed EP200/GL-T in Sicily after its engine was hit.

On 29 August No 1435 Sqn's rising stars Flt Lt Wally McLeod and Sgt Allan Scott knocked down two Bf 109s out of a formation of 15 for the last confirmed victories of the month.

The 29th also marked an important milestone in the development of the Spitfire. With the approval of AVM Park, Wg Cdr Hanks flew the first Spitfire (EP201) modified to carry two 250-lb bombs. Described by No 126 Sqn ace Plt Off Bill Rolls as a 'Heath Robinson arrangement', the weapons were attached to a modified Beaufighter bomb rack. The whole affair was then dropped, leaving a single inch-long rib protruding down from the Spitfire's wing. Soon after BR236 and BR368 were also modified.

With few bombing raids to oppose, the Spitfire units managed to claim only 37 aircraft destroyed in August – the lowest tally for five months. Nevertheless, 13 pilots had been killed in action.

QUIETEST MONTH

September began with a complete lack of aerial activity on the 1st. A C.202 was downed by No 249 Sqn on the 2nd, and three days later future No 185 Sqn ace Flt Lt Ken Charney (in BR375/GL-A) downed the first Bf 109G-2 to be destroyed over Malta when he downed a II./JG 53 machine that he misidentified as a C.202. At 0930 hrs on 9 September No 185 Sqn sent seven Spitfires on a sweep over Sicily. As the fighters neared Biscari, six Bf 109s and a C.202 were spotted. The Macchi was downed by South African pilot Capt Keith Kuhlmann and a Bf 109 was claimed by Sgt Claude Weaver, taking his tally to 10.5 kills.

Weaver was then shot down by a hastily scrambled C.202 piloted by Tenente Paolo Daimani of 352ª *Squadriglia*. The aggressive, extroverted 'Okie' crash-landing on a beach at Scoglitti. The Italians had previously heard his radio chatter, and Weaver was greeted on the scene by his captors with the line 'Hello Claude. How are you?' Following the departure of

Officers from the *Regia Aeronautica* examine BR112/X of No 185 Sqn on the beach at Scoglitti on 9 September 1942, its pilot, Sgt Claude Weaver, having already been taken prisoner (*via Frederick Galea*)

Although records are vague, BR379/T-V of No 249 Sqn probably flew into Malta as part of Operation *Style*, and survived until it was shot down on 4 October 1942 by a Bf 109. Its pilot, Flt Sgt G A Hogarth, was killed. During its career on Malta, the aircraft had been flown by Canadian Sgt Thurne 'Tommy' Parks, who was known for being a tough character. Indeed, he led a revolt en route to Malta protesting about the quality of the food aboard his ship. This got him busted to the rank of corporal. On Malta, with his rank restated, Parks claimed a Bf 109 destroyed and a second fighter damaged flying BR379 on 2 July (*via Frederick Galea*)

'Slim' Yarra in mid-July, Weaver had become No 185 Sqn's top-scoring ace. The unit's combat diary for 8 September recounted:

'On this occasion a half-a-dozen Macchi 202s were run into, and Keith Kuhlman promptly shot one down. "Weave" went down after others, and the last we saw of him, he was sitting on the tail of a Macchi (or '109), which was going down almost vertically. The other "Eyeties" had put their noses down and beat a hasty retreat. As the flight made for home, "Weave" called up on the R/T and told us that he was on fire, and was going to land on the beach – he also mentioned something about stealing a rowing boat and coming back as soon as possible! He claimed an enemy aircraft destroyed. Next day, the Italian radio said their "chasers" had found a British aircraft on land, and that the pilot, an American, had been taken prisoner. They also announced the loss of two Italian aircraft.'

Four Spitfire pilots perished during the course of September, two of whom were killed in action when bounced by Axis fighters on the 15th.

'Screwball' Beurling, who had been grounded through the latter part of August with dysentery, scored his first victories for more than a month on 25 September. Flying EP706/T-L, his was one of ten Spitfires scrambled by No 249 Sqn (along with two from No 1435 Sqn) that rose to intercept 12 Bf 109G-2s from I./JG 77. Proving that Beurling he not lost his touch despite his recent illness, he was the only pilot to succeed in knocking any of the fighters down – the Canadian destroyed two and damaged a third:

'As "Tiger White 2", I attacked two Messerschmitts from a formation of twelve, approaching from starboard quarter above. Fired one-and-a-half-second burst from 300 yards. Enemy aircraft disintegrated. Attacked No 2 aircraft from astern. Two-second burst, 350 yards. Enemy aircraft emitted black smoke from engine, with pieces coming off cowling, then glycol followed afterwards. Attacked third enemy aircraft five minutes later, six miles east of previous position, from port quarter, slightly above, 250–300 yards. Fired two-second burst. Enemy aircraft enveloped in flames, dived vertically, striking the sea. Enemy pilot was seen going down by parachute, and was fired upon by Messerschmitt, causing the parachute to stream.'

Late in the month, Battle of France ace Sqn Ldr Mike Stephens arrived at Luqa. He already had 11.5 kills to his credit, having scored these in Hurricanes in 1940–41 (including two Italian SM.84 bombers downed while on detachment to the Turkish Air Force in 1941). Stephens' recent assignments had been non-operational, however, and it had been a year since he had seen action. He was attached to No 249 Sqn as a supernumery in order to gain experience of local conditions.

Spitfire units claimed just 11 victories during September, which proved to be quietest month of the entire year. Indeed, only 38 alerts were flown in four weeks. Things were about to change, however, for Axis forces planned on making one last attempt to subdue Malta in October.

October also began quietly, although on the 4th I./JG 77 probed the island's defences and downed two pilots from No 249 Sqn – both Flt Sgts M I Gass (in EP700/Q) and G A Hogarth RCAF were killed.

The calm before the storm lasted until 10 October. During September the Luftwaffe had tried to build up its now thinly stretched forces in preparation for yet another offensive against Malta. There was no question of invasion now, as ground troops were no longer available. If Rommel's forces were to prevail in Egypt, however, Malta had to be neutralised. This time, the Luftwaffe had just 156 serviceable Ju 88A-4s, drawn from KGs 54 and 77, and II./LG 1. The fighter element consisted of *Stab.*, I. and II./JG 53 and I./JG 77 with Bf 109F-4/G-2s, as well as I./SchG 2 with Bf 109F-4 *Jabos* – a force totalling 58 serviceable fighters. The *Regia Aeronautica* also had about 100 fighters (C.202s and a small number of Re.2001s) that would escort the Ju 88s in what became known as the 'October *Blitz*'. Italian bombers would not participate in the coming daylight raids over Malta, sticking to night missions instead.

Although there were several notable aces included in the ranks of JG 53 and JG 77, Axis fighter units were now undermanned and understrength, and were flying war-weary aircraft. Even the introduction of the new Bf 109G-2 could not reverse the situation. Just as in the final phase of the Battle of Britain, Axis aircrews were suffering from low morale brought on by fatigue and frustration. And to make matters worse, they would now be opposed by a more robust defence on Malta than had previously been the case – 113 Spitfire VB/Cs split between five seasoned fighter units that were manned by 100 combat-hardened pilots.

Amongst the latter were a handful of highly experienced aces, including Canadians George Beurling, Willie Williams and John McElroy with No 249 Sqn, Britons Bill Rolls, Arthur Varey, American Rip Jones, Canadian Rod Smith and New Zealander Nigel Park of No 126 Sqn, Canadians Wally McLeod, Ian Maclennan and Englishman Allan Scott of No 1435 Sqn, Australian Colin Parkinson and Canadian Jim Ballantyne of No 229 Sqn and Canadian Len Reid of No 185 Sqn.

They were ably led by Wg Cdr Arthur Donaldson at Takali, Wg Cdr Peter Prosser Hanks at Luqa and Wg Cdr John Thompson at Hal Far. At this time No 249 Sqn was commanded by Eric Woods, with Mike Stephens as supernumerary (both were aces), No 229 Sqn had Butch Baker (also an ace) in command, No 126 Sqn had Bryan Wicks, No 1435 Sqn had Sqn Tony Lovell (ace) and No 185 Sqn was led by 'Zulu' Swales. These units were under the able control of Senior Controller Gp Capt A B 'Woody' Woodhall and the leadership of AVM Keith Park

The offensive element now consisted of the Beauforts of No 39 Sqn, Beaufighters of No 227 Sqns, Wellingtons of No 69 Sqn's 'C' Flight and the Swordfish and Albacores of the combined Fleet Air Arm unit.

Six probing attacks were made on 10 October, but Malta's air defence was so effective now that five were intercepted north of the island. During these first incursions, Sqn Ldr Mike Stephens damaged a Bf 109 whilst flying EP140/P-v to open his Malta account and Plt Off Beurling, who was carrying out an air test in EP706/T-L, engaged two German fighters and shot them down.

Australian Colin Henry Parkinson had served briefly with Nos 56 and 19 Sqns prior to being posted to Malta – he flew to the island from *Eagle* in Spitfire BR376 as part of Operation *Salient* on 9 June 1942. Initially a flight sergeant with No 603 Sqn, he claimed a third of a C.202 kill on 23 June, followed by four more victories (all fighters) the following month. Parkinson also claimed four damaged and one probable during this period. Promoted to pilot officer and transferred to No 229 Sqn in early August, he destroyed a Ju 88 on the ground and a Bf 109 in the air during a sweep over Sicily on 27 August, followed by three more kills in the 'October *Blitz*'. Parkinson was tour-expired by December, whereupon he returned to Australia and flew Spitfires with No 457 Sqn RAAF in the defence of Darwin. He claimed no further victories, however (*via Frederick Galea*)

Fifty aircraft, including two Ju 88s, approached at 1040 hrs. Although 23 Spitfires were scrambled, only No 249 Sqn made contact, becoming embroiled in a dogfight with 12 Bf 109s. Several were claimed as damaged or probables, but only Plt Off J G Sanderson and Flg Off John McElroy (in EP708/T-U) got confirmed kills. Another Bf 109 was destroyed later that day, along with more damaged and probables.

Compared with past months, the Allied defenders on Malta were now confident that they could repel any attacks. Their mood was summed up on the evening of 10 October by AVM Park, who stated that the 'Spitfires have won the toss and will keep hard hitting until the match is won.'

The so called 'October *Blitz*' commenced in earnest on the 11th with a raid at 0720 hrs by nine Ju 88s, 25 C.202s and four Bf 109s on Hal Far. Nineteen Spitfires from Nos 1435, 126 and 229 Sqns responded, with aircraft from the latter unit intercepting the enemy at 25,000 ft. Plt Off Jim Stevenson downed a C.202 and Sgt Jack Yeatman claimed a Bf 109 destroyed, while seasoned Canadian ace Flg Off Rod Smith got a Ju 88. This raid caused little damage.

The next attack came over at 1100 hrs, and consisted of six Ju 88s and 65 fighters heading for Luqa. Twenty Spitfires from Nos 185, 229, 1435 and 126 Sqns intercepted them, and during an inconclusive combat several probables and damaged were claimed, but no confirmed kills. On the other hand, the bombing caused minimal damage.

Raid three came in at 1330 hrs, when seven Ju 88s and a large fighter escort attacked Takali and Rabat. Some 28 Spitfires from Nos 185, 229, 1435 and 126 Sqns were scrambled, and they were joined by Wg Cdr Arthur Donaldson, who had been aloft practising his dive-bombing in BR254/T-S. Joining up with No 229 Sqn, he participated in a head-on attack on the bombers and claimed a Ju 88 for his first full kill. Future RCAF ace Sgt Jim Ballantyne of No 229 Sqn also destroyed a Bf 109.

A new slant on Axis operations was demonstrated during the raid at 1700 hrs, when 16 Ju 88s were joined by 17 Re.2001 fighter-bombers from 22° *Gruppo*, escorted by a mixed force of 25 C.202s and Bf 109s. Attacking the radar station at Salina Bay, all their bombs missed. Twenty-five Spitfires from Nos 185, 229 and 126 Sqns were scrambled in response, and the nine fighters from the latter unit, led by veteran ace Wg Cdr Hanks (in BR498/PP-H), intercepted a formation of Bf 109s and C.202s at 27,000 ft north of Comiso.

Hanks claimed one Bf 109 destroyed and a second one damaged and Flt Lt Bill Rolls downed two Re.2001s, although his aircraft (MK-Q) was shot up by two Bf 109s. No 229 Sqn's Flt Lt Eric Glazebrook and Flt Sgt Jim Ballantyne each claimed a Macchi destroyed, while No 185 Sqn, led by Wg Cdr John Thompson (in EP122/JM-T) was credited with the destruction of three Bf 109s – one each to Thompson, Plt Off Len Reid and Sgt Les Gore.

The fifth raid of the day, at 1745 hrs, proved to be the largest, with 30 Ju 88s drawn from KG 54 and

Spitfire VB D-v (almost certainly EP717) was used by Flt Lt Ian Maclennan RCAF of No 1435 Sqn to down two Ju 88s on 11 October 1942. EP717 featured the standard one-letter ID code as worn by fighters from Nos 1435 249 and 229 Sqns at this time. The unit's V code was painted in a smaller size than the individual aircraft letter, and was always applied aft of the roundel (*via Frederick Galea*)

KG 77 attacking Luqa and Hal Far, but without fighter escort. Five Spitfires from No 229 Sqn and four from No 1435 Sqn were scrambled, with the section from the latter unit sighting 15 Ju 88s from 20,000 ft. Diving on them, Flt Lt Wally McLeod (in BS161/U-v) knocked down two bombers. Flt Sgt Ian Maclennan (in EP717/D-v) described the action:

'I climbed and delivered a stern attack, diving down and opening fire from about 100 yards. Return fire was inaccurate. Strikes were observed on the fuselage – also white sheets of flame and pieces flew off, then the aircraft caught fire. As I broke off, I observed three parachutes come out. I then attacked another Ju 88 over the island from very close range and saw strikes on the wings and fuselage. I broke upwards and lost him. Attacked another approximately southeast of the island, this time attacking from astern and above. Flak and return fire was fairly intense and accurate, both of which got me. I got strikes all over the fuselage, and the port engine cowling flew off. I broke away and attacked again, but was out of ammunition. The Ju 88's port engine caught fire and it spread rapidly, the bomber going down into the sea in flames.'

Sgt Tom Kebbel destroyed another bomber in veteran Malta Spitfire AB264/Z-v, which was a survivor of the early air battles in April and May.

Thirty minutes later another unescorted raid was attempted, and several Ju 88s were damaged by No 229 Sqn Spitfires.

Enemy units had been badly mauled on 11 October, and the Spitfire units had suffered minimal casualties in return. Several aircraft had been badly damaged, but only Kiwi Flt Sgt D D MacLean had been killed. He would the first of 13 Spitfire pilots to perish between 11 and 18 October.

There was no let up in the action on the 12th. Indeed, the combat, if anything, was more intense during the five raids that targeted the island. At 0620 hrs, two waves of Ju 88s (totalling 15 bombers) from III./KG 54, escort by 25 Bf 109s and C.202s, headed for Takali and Luqa. Eight No 185 Sqn Spitfires were the first to make contact, with South African Capt Keith Kuhlmann (in EP187) being credited with a Bf 109 destroyed. Others claimed several damaged.

The first wave of bombers pressed on and succeeded in bombing both airfields, but they inflicted only minimal damage on aircraft at Luqa. They were hurried on their way by ten No 249 Sqn Spitfires, and several were damaged and one Ju 88 shared destroyed by Sgt Al Stead (in EP199/K) and Sqn Ldr Mike Stephens (AB377/T-E), who then managed to shoot down a second Bf 109. Suddenly finding himself alone, Stephens was bounced by another German fighter and forced to bale out. He was quickly rescued by a seaplane tender on what was turning out to be a busy day for the Air Sea Rescue service.

The second wave of Ju 88s bombed Hal Far, destroying a Spitfire and damaging others. However, four were claimed shot down by No 126 Sqn – two by Sgt Nigel Park (in BR311/MK-L) and one each by Flt Lt Bill Rolls (in BR498/PP-H) and Flt Sgt Carl Long. These successes were offset by the loss of Sqn Ldr Wicks (in BR377). Flt Lt Rolls recalled:

'I saw one of the Ju 88s I had fired at diving down, and I put a final burst into it and it almost fell to pieces. I followed to 4000 ft and thought I saw two bale out. I did not see what happened to the others I hit, as I was too busy getting out of the mass of aircraft flying around. I saw Ju 88s burning and going down all over the place. I had reached the outside of

Sqn Ldr Mike Stephens had already enjoyed an eventful war before he even reached Malta. Having 'made ace' during the Battle of France with No 3 Sqn, he then undertook a variety of postings in the Middle East that included seeing combat with the Turkish Air Force in 1941 and briefly flying with the USAAF's 57th FG in Egypt. Posted as a supernumerary squadron leader to Malta, he was in the thick of the final 'October *Blitz*', adding seven more victories to his tally flying with Nos 249 and 229 Sqns – he led the latter unit from 13 October until made leader of the Hal Far Wing the following month. Stephens ended the war with 22 victories to his name (*via Frederick Galea*)

the melee when I saw a Spitfire going down. I flew up to it and saw it was my CO. He was injured by the looks of it. I watched him bale out and saw his 'chute open. After what seemed ages he hit the water and his "Mae West" was supporting him, but there was no sign of life.'

CO of No 126 Sqn since August, Bryan Wicks had claimed four kills flying Hurricanes with No 56 Sqn during 1940. He was the only squadron commander of a Spitfire unit to be killed defending Malta.

The second raid of the day came over at 0910 hrs, consisting of seven Ju 88s from III./KG 54, with close escort by C.202s and Bf 109s operating in a free hunt role. Eight No 229 Sqn Spitfires intercepted them 30 miles north of Gozo, the unit being led in by Wg Cdr Donaldson (in BR529/AD). Sgt Ballantyne claimed a C.202 and Donaldson shared a Ju 88 with Plt Off H G Reynolds. While this was going on, No 249 Sqn 'mixed it up' with the Bf 109s of II./JG 53, which were stepped in formation from 21,000 ft up to 30,000 ft. Flg Off John McElroy was able to destroy one, and several others were claimed as probables and damaged, after which the Germans broke off combat.

A section of No 126 Sqn attacked the retreating bombers from the first wave north of Gozo, and this resulted in Flt Lt Bill Rolls adding two C.202s to his earlier Ju 88 claim, Sgt Nigel Park got his third Ju 88 of the day (to 'make ace') and Flg Off E W Wallace downed a bomber.

Fifteen miles north of Grand Harbour, No 1435 Sqn engaged the second wave of six Ju 88s, which had a close escort of Macchis and an indirect escort of Messerschmitts. Flg Sgt Maclennan managed to shoot down a Bf 109 while flying EP203/G-v, but Sgt Kebbell was shot down in BR368/I-v, successfully baling out. The Ju 88s were intercepted over Takali by eight of No 185 Sqn's Spitfires, and Sgt John Vinall (in EP139) was shot down and killed by the bombers' Bf 109 escorts. Some of the Ju 88s were damaged but none were shot down.

At 1200 hrs the third raid of the day approached – eight Ju 88s, with an escort of ten C.202s and 20 Bf 109s. As was routine now, they were attacked just south of Sicily. Leading in the intercepting force of eight No 249 Sqn Spitfires and seven fighters from No 229 Sqn was Wg Cdr Donaldson (in BR529/AD), who immediately damaged one bomber and shot down another. Sqn Ldr Eric Woods of No 249 Sqn dove in with Flg Off John McElroy (in AR488/T-R) and Flt Sgt Hiskens, and the latter two each claimed a Ju 88 destroyed. Woods added a Bf 109 to this. Flt Lt Glazebrook of No 229 Sqn downed a Ju 88, while squadronmates Plt Colin Parkinson (in EP691/X-A) and Flt Sgt Jim Ballantyne each claimed a Bf 109 destroyed.

The fighters had downed four bombers and four fighters, claimed two bombers and a fighter as probables and damaged three fighters and two bombers, all without loss. To add to the woes of the Germans, six

No 229 Sqn Spitfire VB EP691/X-A was flown in combat by Plt Off Colin Parkinson RAAF on 11, 12 and 13 October 1942, during which time he downed a Bf 109 and claimed other aircraft damaged or as probables. EP691 well illustrates the wear and tear inflicted on Malta Spitfires. It is thought to have been flown into Malta on 17 August 1942 as part of Operation *Baritone* (*via Frederick Galea*)

No 1435 Sqn aircraft joined the fight, taking on Bf 109s north of Grand Harbour. Flt Lt McLeod shot a Bf 109 off the tail of his wingman.

A different formula was tried on the next raid at 1445 hrs, the Axis formation consisting of 23 C.202s and eight Bf 109s escorting 23 Re.2001 fighter-bombers. Again the Spitfires were scrambled, six from No 229 Sqn, eight from No 185 Sqn and nine from No 126 Sqn. Wg Cdr Hanks led in a section from the latter unit, attacking Bf 109s at 23,000 ft. They were in turn bounced by four more fighters, but Hanks managed to down one of their assailants. No Spitfires were lost.

Raid five was intercepted halfway to Malta at 1530 hrs, eight Ju 88s and 57 Bf 109s being countered by eight Spitfires from No 1435 Sqn, with Sqn Ldr Tony Lovell in the lead (in AR470/Q-v). He claimed one Ju 88 destroyed, while future ace Flt Sgt Allan Scott (in EP203/G-v) downed a Bf 109 (recorded as an 'Re.2001' by his unit) and a Ju 88 probable. Flt Sgt Ron Stevenson (in EP209/B-v) failed to return, however.

By dusk on 12 October, Malta's Spitfire units had claimed 27 Axis aircraft destroyed (12 Ju 88s, 11 Bf 109s, three C.202s and one Re.2001) and 13 probables and damaged at a cost of seven Spitfires destroyed, three pilots killed and one seriously wounded – six fighters had also been damaged. These figures represented the highest number of claims made in a single day by the defenders during the entire siege. As such, 12 October 1942 could be looked upon as the apex of the entire battle, although the offensive would continue for a few more days.

Action on the 13th proved that the Axis air forces had not yet given up. At 0635 hrs, the first raid of the day came in the form of seven Ju 88s, with an escort of 30 Bf 109s. Eight Spitfires from No 185 Sqn made contact first, and several enemy aircraft were claimed as probables and damaged – two Spitfires were also damaged – but no kills were confirmed by the unit. No 249 Sqn then engaged the formation, with Flt Lt Eric Hetherington (in AR466/T-R) leading eight Spitfires against the bombers three miles north of St Paul's Bay. In short order Plt Off George Beurling (BR173/T-D) damaged a Ju 88 and then destroyed two Bf 109s:

'As "Tiger Red 3", I attacked eight Ju 88s, taking a straggler from slightly above to the right with a two-second burst of cannon and machine guns. Pieces came off the starboard wing. I broke to port and down, and saw a Messerschmitt closing in from port above. I broke left and then turned into him. At 50 yards astern I fired a one-and-a-half-second burst of cannon and machine guns. Enemy aircraft burst into flames. A second Messerschmitt came down from starboard quarter above. As enemy aircraft pulled out ahead at 250–300 yards, I gave him a four-second burst with machine guns – observed no strikes, but pilot baled out. At this time I saw first enemy aircraft strike the sea.'

Some of the bombers hit Luqa, then sped north. Beurling caught one:

'I attacked a Ju 88 from starboard quarter above, 300 yards, with cannon and machine guns, two-second burst, and observed strikes on roots of starboard wing and black, oily smoke poured out. I gave it the remainder of my ammunition into the fuselage. Enemy aircraft did a diving turn to the right, striking the sea.'

Several of the damaged Ju 88s still managed to reach Luqa and drop their bombs, killing two civilians. As the bombers withdrew, Beurling managed to catch up with one and pepper it with shells – the Ju 88 refused

George Beurling was undoubtedly the highest-scoring Allied fighter pilot during the siege of Malta with 27 individual victories and one shared confirmed during the siege. His closest competitor amongst Malta's defenders was 'Paddy' Schade of No 126 Sqn with 13.5 victories. Indeed, Beurling outscored the top Axis pilot of the campaign, Hauptmann Gerhard Michalski of II./JG 53, who claimed 26 victories. This was probably one of only two occasions in which an Allied pilot out-scored his Luftwaffe counterpart in an aerial campaign in World War 2, the other occasion being the Greek campaign in 1941, which saw South African Sqn Leader 'Pat' Pattle far out-score all Axis fighter pilots. After Malta, Beurling transferred to the RCAF and flew with Nos 403 and 412 Sqns over northwest Europe. He gained two further victories over Fw 190s flying Spitfire IXs, bringing his final tally to 31 individual and 1 shared victory claims and 9 damaged. Allowed to 'retire' from the RCAF in October 1944 after numerous run ins with his superiors, Beurling had a difficult time adjusting to civilian life. When news reached him that the fledgling state of Israel was looking for former fighter pilots, he jumped at the chance. Once hired, he ended up at Urbe airport, in Rome, tasked with flying a Norduyn Norseman loaded with arms to Israel. On 20 May 1948, as he took off, his Norseman caught fire and crashed, killing both Beurling and his co-pilot. It has been suggested that sabotage was the cause of the fire (via Frederick Galea)

to go down, however. The bombers were intercepted as they headed north by eight No 1435 Sqn Spitfires, and emerging ace Plt Off Wally Walton (in EP140/P-v) destroyed one, while three others were damaged.

The second raid of the day approached at mid-morning, with six Ju 88s, 28 C.202s and 36 Bf 109s again heading for Luqa. Sixteen Spitfires from Nos 126 and 1435 Sqns intercepted the bombers north of Malta, with Wg Cdr Hanks (in BR498/PP-H) in the lead. As they went after the bombers, they were cut off by the Bf 109s, and only Sgt R Hawkins (in EP259/L-v) shot one down – Flt Sgt Alan Scott got a Bf 109 for his fifth kill. The bombers pressed on and hit the airfield.

Luqa was also the target for the day's third raid, mounted in the early afternoon – six Ju 88s escorted by 25 C.202s and 40 Bf 109s. Eight No 185 Sqn Spitfires intercepted the bombers, but they were in turn bounced by the Bf 109 escort and Sgt Alex MacLeod was shot down and killed (in EP316). Again several bombers were damaged but no confirmed claims were made. Two Spitfires were also damaged in crash-landings. As the Ju 88s returned north, they were pursued by Nos 126 and 185 Sqns. Catching them north of Zonqor Point, the latter unit's Maj 'Zulu' Swales (in EP685) downed a Ju 88 from II./LG 1 with the help of Flt Sgt Varey. No 126 Sqn ace Flg Off 'Rip' Jones also destroyed a Bf 109 and Flg Off Rod Smith got a C.202, making him an ace.

The last raid of the day was detected a short while later when seven Ju 88s, escorted by no fewer than 30 C.202s and 42 Bf 109s, targeted the airfield at Qrendi. Eight Spitfires from No 249 Sqn were scrambled, intercepting the bombers 20 miles to the north of Gozo. Sqn Ldr Mike Stephens (in EP338/A) was the first to make a claim, downing one of the Ju 88s. The fighter escort then intervened, and four of their number were claimed shot down by Sqn Ldr Woods' section. The CO got two Bf 109s (in AR466/T-R), while Flt Sgt Hiskens (in EP135/T-Z) and Flg Off McElroy (in EP340/T-M) each downed a C.202. Sqn Ldr Stephens also claimed a share in a Macchi with Flt Sgt de l'Ara (in BR565/T-T).

At this point No 229 Sqn waded in, with Plt Off H T Nash claiming a Ju 88 shot down. Wg Cdr Donaldson damaged another bomber before his own aircraft (BR539/AD) was shot up and he was forced to crash-land at Luqa. As the Ju 88s retreated, they found themselves having to

Wg Cdr Peter Prosser Hanks saw much action in Spitfire BR498/PP-H in October, as did Flt Lt Bill Rolls of No 126 Sqn, who claimed five victories with it – Hanks got four (*via Frederick Galea*)

Peter Prosser Hanks was a highly experienced fighter pilot by the time he was posted to Malta in early August 1942, having seen plenty of combat flying Hurricanes in the Battle of France with No 1 Sqn, where he gained seven victories. He took command of the Luqa Wing, with Nos 126 and 1435 Sqns, in September 1942, and was able to add four more victories to his tally during the 'October *Blitz*', taking his wartime total to 13 kills (*via Frederick Galea*)

deal with the attentions of No 1435 Sqn, whose Sgt W R Whitmore (in EN968/H-v) downed one. Ace Flt Lt Wally McLeod also got a C.202. This brought the total of destroyed claims for the day to 20.

Although actual German losses were not as high as the figure claimed by the defenders, they were substantial enough for Feldmarschall Kesselring to break off the offensive after just 72 hours in order to conserve his forces for the expected Anglo-American landings in northwest Africa the following month. Attacks would continue for several more days, however, but it was apparent that Malta's fighter defences were too strong for the Axis air forces to deal with.

Kesselring may have abandoned the campaign, but on 14 October Axis bombers still appeared over Malta just as they had done on a daily basis since the 11th. The first raid came in at 0700 hrs, and eight Ju 88s and their escort of 40 fighters had already crossed the coast by the time eight Spitfires from No 249 Sqns attacked them head-on. After damaging a bomber, Donaldson was set upon by a Bf 109, who gained strikes on his cockpit and engine. Hit by splinters in his face, torso, arms and legs, and having lost two fingers, the veteran pilot was left bleeding profusely from his wounds. He decided to risk landing his Spitfire (BR130) at Takali, gliding it in and performing a wheels-up landing to good effect.

Despite the best efforts of No 249 Sqn, the bombers reached Takali just as eight No 185 Sqn Spitfires engaged their escorts. Several Axis fighters were damaged, but none went down. Eight No 126 Sqn aircraft chased the bomber formation away from Malta, and this time the Bf 109s intervened less successfully. One Ju 88 was claimed destroyed by Flt Lt Rolls in Wg Cdr Hanks' BR498/PP-H, Sgt Nigel Park downed a Bf 109 and a Ju 88 and Flg Off E W Wallace got a Messerschmitt fighter. A single No 126 Sqn Spitfire was shot down, but its pilot was rescued.

The second raid of the day (seven Ju 88s, 45 Bf 109s and 29 C.202s) arrived at mid-morning, and first contact was made 20 miles north of Grand Harbour by No 1435 Sqn. Although outnumbered, Flt Lt Wally McLeod downed a Ju 88 just after it had released its bombs, but the unit had Sgts Bill Knox-Williams RAAF and Ronnie Roe RNZAF killed.

No 185 Sqn attacked next, with Wg Cdr Thompson leading in eight Spitfires. Flying his usual mount (EP122/JM-T), Thompson downed a Ju 88, but the remaining bombers managed to reach Hal Far and Safi, where their bombs did little damage. They were then pursued home by No 185 Sqn, whose Capt Kulhmann and Plt Off Reid both downed Bf 109s. No 229 Sqn also engaged the bombers and despatched a Ju 88.

The next raid of the day (seven Ju 88s and a large fighter escort) was detected at 1310 hrs. No 126 Sqn was first in with seven aircraft at 20,000 ft, whereupon Sgt Nigel Park found that his guns were frozen, so he immediately dove to 10,000 ft. The problem soon disappeared in the warmer air, and he was able to add a Bf 109 to his rapidly mounting score. Next up was No 229 Sqn, which encountered the formation at 17,000 ft, and still short of the coast. Flt Lt Colin Parkinson destroyed a C.202 and Sqn Ldr Mike Stephens damaged a Ju 88, before downing an Re.2001.

The Ju 88s now attracted the attention of No 249 Sqn, whose Plt Off K C M Giddings damaged two bombers before shooting down a Bf 109. Plt Off George Beurling (in BR173/T-D) also turned in a stellar performance in what turned out to be his last combat over the island.

An ignominous end for No 249 Sqn Spitfire VB T-M (serial unknown). This incident took place at Takali some time in October 1942 (*via Bruce Robertson*)

Zooming up to 24,000 ft above the Ju 88s, he dove on the formation and downed one with a two-second burst, although he was in turn wounded in the forearm by return fire. With pursing Bf 109s on his tail, he shot a Messerschmitt off the tail of Flt Lt E L Hetherington from 450 yards, then destroyed a Bf 109 that was pursuing Plt Off 'Willie the Kid' Williams. Moments later, Beurling's fighter was hit again by another Bf 109 and the ace was wounded in the right heel and peppered with shrapnel in his left leg. Baling out from 1000 ft, he was picked up by the rescue launch HSL 128. These wounds ended Beurling's Malta career.

He would spend the next two weeks in hospital, where he received news that he had been awarded the Distinguished Service Order. Beurling was also told to pack up and get ready to go home for a bond tour. Angry at being declared tour-expired, he stated during his farewell party that he would rather fly for the Germans than be a 'prisoner' in Canada.

The final raid on 14 October came in at 1630 hrs, and consisted of eight Ju 88s, 44 Bf 109s and 31 C.202s. Intercepted by ten No 126 Sqn Spitfires led by Wg Cdr Hanks whilst still over the sea, the bomber crews panicked and immediately jettisoned their ordnance. This did not prevent five of them from being claimed shot down by Flg Off R Smith, Plt Off W I Thompson, Flt Sgt A Varey and Sgts W Marshall and P Charon. No 229 Sqn also attacked this formation head-on, and Sgt R Miller claimed a kill.

As the bombers turned for Sicily, they were intercepted by eight No 185 Sqn Spitfires, whose Flt Sgt E L Mahar claimed yet another Ju 88 destroyed. The engagement now turned into a swirling fighter-versus-fighter clash, and Wt Off G H T Farquharson of No 126 downed a Bf 109 – no Spitfires were lost. German records suggest that only one bomber was destroyed in this action, but it cannot be ignored that the Ju 88s had jettisoned their bombs and beat a hasty retreat.

On 15 October, an early morning raid on Luqa by six Ju 88s and their fighter escort managed to avoid being intercepted until they were actually over their target. Sqn Ldr Tony Lovell, at the head of eight No 1435 Sqn Spitfires, caught the raiders pulling out of their dives over Kalafrana Bay. Flt Off Wally Walton (in EP140/P-v) shot a Ju 88 down and Flt Sgt Allan Scott claimed a Bf 109 (in BP873/Y-v).

Eight No 249 Sqn Spitfires lay waiting for the raiders north of Zonqor Point, but they were in turn attacked by the Bf 109 escorts. American Sgt Vassure 'Georgia' Wynn managed to shoot one of the fighters down (in BR373/T-N). The bombers were then engaged, with Plt Off V K Moody destroying one (in EP135/T-Z). The Ju 88s continued to be harassed as they headed out to sea by a section of fighters from No 229 Sqn, who

Sgt Vassure 'Georgia' Wynn of No 249 Sqn hailed from Dalton, Georgia, and was one of a significant number of Americans who served in the defence of Malta either as members of the RAF or, as in Wynn's case, the RCAF. Transferring in June 1943 to the USAAF, he gained 2.5 victories with the famed 4th FG. Remaining in the USAF post-war, he later claimed a MiG-15 damaged over Korea. Wynn's total for World War 2 was three solo kills (one on Malta) and two shared by war's end. He is seen here about to get into his No 249 Sqn Spitfire. Note its freshly applied paint (*IWM*)

were also joined by some No 1435 Sqn aircraft. Sqn Ldr Mike Stephens chased two Ju 88s for 35 minutes before downing one, and he then turned into six pursuing Bf 109s and promptly destroyed one of them too – even though his own aircraft (BR562/X-R) was damaged. He escaped his assailants and crash-landed at Takali.

Not to be left out, No 126 Sqn, led by Flt Lt 'Rip' Jones, also engaged the escorts, and he and Flt Lt Arthur Varey claimed a Bf 109 kill apiece. However, they both probably claimed the fighter flown by II./JG 53's *Gruppenkommandeur*, Hauptmann Gerhard Michalski (the Luftwaffe's ranking Malta ace). Baling out, he was rescued by a Do 24 flying boat.

As with the previous four days, a raid appeared at mid-morning, consisting of eight Ju 88s, eight Bf 109 *Jabos* and an escort of 25 C.202s, with Bf 109s as high cover. This time the mere appearance of 15 Spitfires from Nos 1435 and 249 Sqns caused the *Jabos* to jettison their bombs. The Spitfires were, however, bounced by the escorting Bf 109s, and an inconclusive dogfight ensued. While this was going on, a section from No 126 Sqn spotted two Bf 109s attempting to cover the rescue of Hauptmann Michalski, and one of the German fighters was downed by Wg Cdr Hanks (in BR498/PP-H).

At 1200 hrs, 50 fighters approached the island, apparently escorting an Air Sea Rescue flying boat. They were intercepted by No 1435 Sqn and two C.202s were downed. At much the same time, another sweep was made by 30 Axis fighters, seven of which were carrying bombs. No 1435 Sqn, which was still airborne, was joined by Nos 126 and 249 Sqns as the German aircraft were engaged. In a sign of apparent fatigue on both sides, the *Jabos* missed their mark and No 126 Sqn survived being bounced by No 249 Sqn. Another abortive *Jabo* attack was attempted at noon.

It was back to business as usual in the mid-afternoon, when six Ju 88s, escorted by 61 Bf 109s and C.202s, were intercepted by No 249 Sqn. The unit was led by Sqn Ldr Eric Woods, who noticed the bombers jettisoning their loads as they approached. He gained strikes on no fewer than four of the Ju 88s, then downed a Bf 109 with a two-second burst from just 100 yards. A second German fighter was downed by Flg Off McElroy (in BR373/T-N). However, Australian Wt Off Ted Hiskens fell prey to one of the escorts, being shot down and killed in (EP340/T-M). No 185 Sqn also joined the attack and a Ju 88 was also destroyed. McElroy's Spitfire had by then been shot up, and he just managed to crash-land at Takali.

The Luftwaffe claimed to have inflicted severe damage on Takali on 15 October, but in reality not a single bomb had hit the base. The RAF claimed 13 Axis aircraft destroyed in return.

Another early morning raid was attempted on 16 October, with eight Ju 88s and a large fighter escort approaching soon after dawn. As 23 Spitfires from Nos 126, 185 and 1435 Sqns approached, several bombers again jettisoned their loads in the sea off Zonqor. No 126 Sqn made contact first, with Flt Lt Bill Rolls (in BR498/PP-H) downing a Ju 88. Two probables and two damaged were claimed by the other two units. However, the Bf 109s put up quite a fight, and Flg Off Ed Wallace RCAF of No 126 Sqn and Sgt Bill Wilson of No 1435 Sqn were both killed. Their deaths were partially avenged by Sgt Nigel Park, who claimed a Bf 109 for his ninth Malta victory.

Sqn Ldr Eric 'Timber' Woods flew into Malta off HMS *Furious* as part of Operation *Bellows* on 11 August 1942. Taking command of No 249 Sqn at Takali, he led the unit throughout the 'October *Blitz*'. Between 12 and 15 October he scored five confirmed victories, one probable and three damaged. His total score on Malta came to 7.666 destroyed and 1 destroyed on the ground. Woods' overall wartime score stood at 11.666 when he was killed in a mid-air collision with his wingman over Yugoslavia on 16 December 1943 whilst serving as CO of No 286 Wing (*via Frederick Galea*)

The second raid of the day came in not long after the previous one, and this time it penetrated the fighter defence. While No 1435 Sqn skirmished with Bf 109s, seven Ju 88s escorted by 50 fighters tried to dive-bomb Hal Far. Eight No 229 Sqn Spitfires attempted to intercept them, but they were in turn mauled by the Messerschmitts, losing one Spitfire shot down and another forced to crash-land. One Ju 88 had been destroyed and two damaged prior to the Bf 109s' intervention. Six Spitfires of No 249 Sqn caught the bombers as they were going into their dives over Hal Far, and one was downed and several damaged. However, Flt Sgt Peter Carter RCAF was shot down (in EP338/T-A) and killed by Feldwebel Golinski of 3./JG 53, who was in turn despatched by Flt Lt Wally McLeod (in EP451/Q-v) – the ace's aircraft was damaged moments later, forcing him to crash-land at Luqa.

A third raid of the day was a pointless affair in which Bf 109 fighter-bombers and their escort managed to avoid interception, only to then drop their bombs harmlessly in an open field.

At 1600 hrs seven Ju 88s, with an escort of 42 C.202s and 40 Bf 109s, entered Maltese airspace in six waves, eluded the Spitfires and bombed Luqa and Takali. Flt Lt Hetherington led eight of No 249 Sqn's Spitfires in a head-on attack on the bombers as they reached open water, and Plt Off Williams claimed a Ju 88 and Plt Off Sanderson a Bf 109 destroyed. Nos 126 and 229 Sqns then entered the fray and destroyed a Ju 88 apiece.

During the early hours of the following morning (17th), a new draft of replacement pilots flew into Malta from Gibraltar aboard a Hudson. The 17th would also mark the end of the limited Luftwaffe/*Regia Aeronautica* offensive.

At 0645 hrs Sqn Ldr Tony Lovell led a section of No 1435 Sqn fighters in a head-on attack on seven Ju 88s. They failed to knock any of the bombers down, so eight more Spitfires from No 126 Sqn followed suit and promptly destroyed three Ju 88s. Wg Cdr Hanks (in BR498/PP-H), Flg Off Stevenson and Plt Off Thompson each claimed one apiece, and Flt Sgt Varey also downed a Bf 109. This success came at a high price, however, for Flt Lt 'Rip' Jones (in EP341) collided head-on with a Ju 88 and was killed. The ex-US Navy pilot from New York was one of the leading aces in No 126 Sqn, having seven and two shared victories to his credit at the time of his death.

Axis tactics had changed on this day, with the Germans and Italians now attacking from several directions at once. Even though some aircraft reached their targets, they failed to score a knock out blow on the airfields due to inaccurate bombing.

Off schedule, the noon raid was ten minutes late on the 17th. It consisted of eight Ju 88s, nine Bf 109 *Jabos* and an escort of no less than 41 Bf 109s and 31 C.202s. Due to a sluggish response by the defenders, the bombers all got through. However, the *Jabos'* attack on Takali

Pictured here are two stalwarts of No 249 Sqn, Flg Off John McElroy and Flg Off Eric Hetherington. During July, McElroy scored two and one shared destroyed, five damaged and two probables. He was very much to the fore during the 'October *Blitz*', downing a Bf 109 on 10 October, followed by two Bf 109s on the 12th, an Re.2001 on the 13th and a Ju 88 on the 15th. A shared Bf 109 on 22 October brought total credits on the island to seven and two shared destroyed, 11 and one shared damaged and two probables. After the war, he volunteered for the fledgling Israeli Air Force and downed three more aircraft, including two RAF Spitfires. Eric Hetherington frequently flew with George Beurling, and claimed 3.333 victories over Malta. He was killed in the Liberator crash at Gibraltar on 31 October 1942 (*via Patrick Lee*)

caused little damage, and the Ju 88s' bombs fell wide, damaging several civilian houses. Two bombers were subsequently destroyed by Spitfires from Nos 249 and 126 Sqns, with one of the aircraft carrying the *Gruppenkommandeur* of II./LG 1 to his death. Three Bf 109s were also claimed shot down, one of these being the last victory for Australian ace Flt Lt Colin Parkinson of No 229 Sqn. Sadly, his friend Flt Sgt Ron 'Dusty' Miller was killed in Spitfire BP955/X-A during this engagement.

As if to demonstrate that the Axis offensive was all but over, the following day an Italian bomb group approached the island with an escort of 50 fighters. The bombers steered clear of Malta, however, choosing instead to drop their bombs in open water and head for home. As per usual, the Bf 109s put up a stiff fight, and one was shot down by No 126 Sqn. However, the unit's Flg Off J D Stevenson RCAF was killed and Sgt Nigel Park was forced to crash-land EP345/MK-X at Luqa.

The Luftwaffe and *Regia Aeronautica* had indeed thrown in the towel on the 18th and conceded defeat. After this day there would be occasional fighter sweeps and reconnaissance sorties, but the heat was off Malta.

The 'October *Blitz*' more than any other series of air battles in the long siege of Malta represented the climax and end of the campaign by the Axis powers to take the island. Although there would be more air combat, it would be on a much reduced scale, as the focus was now on supporting the *Afrika Korps*. Indeed, on the 19th Axis air forces halted the Malta campaign altogether. This day could be seen as the end of the air battle for the central Mediterranean. A sense of futility had permeated Axis bomber and fighter units, especially those that had served the longest on Sicily – they were said to be afflicted with 'Malta sickness'. Now began the long winding down of the Malta campaign.

During the nine days of the 'October *Blitz*', the Luftwaffe and *Regia Aeronautica* had flown approximately 2400 sorties and dropped 440 tons of bombs. In spite of this, no airfield was out of operation for more than 30 minutes, and on average there were 74 Spitfires serviceable each day. The Spitfire units had generated 1115 sorties and lost 30 aircraft and 14 pilots in response to the enemy raids.

On 20 and 21 October heavy rain fell on Malta, rendering the waterlogged prone Luqa inoperable – something Axis bombers had failed to do during the previous week. Between 22 and 25 October, veterans like McLeod, McElroy, Smith and Williams all scored single kills, but there was far less Axis activity than in previous months.

On 25 October came the loss of 10.25-victory ace Sgt Nigel 'Tiger' Park RNZAF, who also happened to be the nephew of AVM Keith Park. That day, 15 C.202s escorted three Re.2001 fighter-bombers that had attempted to bomb Takali – there were an unknown number of Bf 109 fighters and *Jabos* also taking part in this raid. One of the intercepting units was 'B' flight of No 126 Sqn, led by Flt Lt Bill Rolls (in BR345/MK-S). After an inconclusive fight, it was discovered on landing that the 21-year-old Kiwi was missing. It was thought that he went down with his aircraft (BR311/MK-L) after destroying a Bf 109, as related by Bill Rolls:

'I was told by one of the pilots that he had seen "Parky's" aircraft hit the sea, and he thought he had seen a parachute coming from it. Someone else had seen a Spitfire crash into the sea, but that it went down with the pilot still in it. I hastily rang the ASR, and they told me they had the

New Zealander Nigel Park was the nephew of AVM Keith Park. Upon joining the RNZAF, he was sent to the UK and eventually arrived on Malta after flying off *Eagle* on 15 July 1942. He joined No 126 Sqn at Luqa, and claimed his first two kills on 28 July (a Bf 109 and a shared Ju 88). This was followed by another Bf 109 on 9 August. During the 'October *Blitz*' Park destroyed three Ju 88s on 12 October, two Bf 109s and a Ju 88 on the 14th and a Bf 109 on the 16th. He was killed in action on 25 October, having been credited with a Bf 109 destroyed in his final flight (in BR311/L-MK) (*via Frederick Galea*)

information, but that it would take some time to get there and it would be getting dark soon. I rang Operations to ask permission to go out and search for "Parky", or to protect him if he was in his dinghy. We took off for that area, which we searched for almost an hour before it started to get dark and we had to return to base and leave it to the ASR.'

Also on this day, the first two of 12 Spitfires flew directly from Gibraltar to Malta thanks to the fitment of 170-gallon slipper fuel tanks under the belly and a 29-gallon tank behind the cockpit. The forerunners of things to come, they arrived safely after a 5.25-hour flight.

On 26 October, in the last notable combat for the month, there were three incursions made by Axis fighters. An early morning fighter sweep by 35 fighters resulted in a victory claim for Canadian Plt Off Ian Maclennan in (BR591/R-v). A further sweep at 1030 hrs was intercepted by a flight of No 126 Sqn Spitfires, and after disrupting the fighter-bombers, Flt Lt Bill Rolls and his wingman caught two Messerschmitts at 8000 ft. Flying BR345/MK-S, Rolls damaged one and fired on the other fighter with machine guns only – he was credited with a Bf 109 destroyed. This brought his total for the war to 17, of which 8.5 were claimed on Malta. During the last Axis fighter sweep of the day, Plt Off Wally Walton claimed a Bf 109 destroyed (in EP188/G-v). This took the tally of kills claimed by the Malta Spitfire units in October to 144.5.

The 29th saw the very last carrier fly-off of Spitfires to Malta, Operation *Train* covering the delivery of 29 fighters from *Furious*. And with the recent infusion of new pilots, the defence was in very good shape.

With bombing raids suspended, the Luftwaffe reverted to a tactic it had tried in the last months of 1940 after defeat in the Battle of Britain. Fighter sweeps and small-scale fighter-bomber raids were generated in an effort to draw the Spitfires into the air for their supposed destruction. As in 1940 on the Channel Front, these missions were not effective.

On 31 October there was a tragic end for some of those who had survived the siege. Twenty-four tour-expired or wounded pilots (including Plt Off Beurling, with his foot in a plaster cast as a result of the wound he received on the 14th) and ten civilians were evacuated from Malta aboard a Liberator bound for the UK. The No 511 Sqn aircraft had earlier arrived from Alexandria, bringing in Sqn Ldrs Tommy Smart and Jack Urwin-Mann to take command of Nos 229 and 126 Sqns, respectively.

Having refuelled, the transport departed Malta at 0300 hrs, heading for its next stop, Gibraltar. Aside from Beurling, other notable pilots included Arthur Donaldson, Eric Hetherington, Arthur Varey and John 'Willie the Kid' Williams. Unfortunately, as they arrived at Gibraltar in the midst of a severe storm, the pilot overshot the runway and the aircraft stalled into the sea 100 yards from shore as he attempted to go around again. Eight civilians and six pilots were killed, either through drowning or of injuries sustained in the crash. Sadly, amongst those to die were Beurling's close friends Eric Hetherington, who was his most frequent wingman, and fellow Canadian John Williams. As Beurling later recalled:

'I'd never go roaring up to 28,000 ft again with "Hether", both of us proud as hell that we could beat any team in 249 to get up where the Jerries were. I'd never wipe another Hun off "Willie's" tail, or bawl him out for cruising around watching a flamer spiral down. There wasn't any "Hether" and there wasn't any "Willie".'

Bill Rolls emerged as one of the leading RAF aces in the early years of the war. Having joined the RAFVR shortly before the outbreak of the war, he was initially posted to No 72 Sqn in June 1940 and saw much combat during the Battle of Britain, scoring seven kills. Rolls flew another tour with No 122 Sqn in 1941–42, scoring 1.5 Fw 190 kills. In July 1942 he was posted overseas, flying off *Furious* on 11 August during the *Pedestal* operation. He was posted to No 126 Sqn as a flight leader, and downed a Ju 88 on 13 August and a Do 24 on 19 September, followed by six victories during the 'October *Blitz*'. Rolls downed one more victory (a Bf 109) on 26 October, then accidentally broke his foot and spent the remainder of his time in Malta in hospital. He was then posted back to the UK and performed non-operational duties for the rest of the war (*via Frederick Galea*)

AFTERMATH

The month of November saw the sharp drop off in aerial combat continue, with few opportunities for Malta's Spitfire units to add to their scores. The Axis air forces were now resorting to sporadic token *Jabo* raids, which were in general met in force by the now full strength air defence units. The last five of 12 long-range Spitfire VCs were flown into Luqa from Gibraltar on 6 November, and this was the final reinforcement flight sent to the island – another milestone signifying that the siege was over.

As the Luftwaffe tried to supply German and Italian forces in Tunisia, there was increased offensive aerial activity for the Malta fighter wings as they attempted to intercept enemy transports flying between Sicily and North Africa. Just such a target presented veteran Malta ace Plt Off Ian Maclennan with the last of his seven victory claims on Malta on 14 November when he shot down one of two SM.82 transports claimed by No 1435 Sqn. Earlier in the day, future ace Plt Off Jesse Hibbert had scored his first kill when he downed a Ju 52/3m in EP433/N-v flying with No 126 Sqn. This was his only Malta victory, and he would later achieve ace status over northwest Europe in 1944–45.

November was the quietest month yet on Malta, with only five victories being claimed by the Spitfire units.

Malta strikes back: Wg Cdr John Thompson (AR560/JMT) is seen leading a 'Spit-bomber' strike from Luqa against a Sicilian target in early 1943. With the lifting of the siege, raids against Sicily were the order of the day. These Spitfires all carry a single 250-lb bomb beneath each wing (*IWM*)

In December, in an effort to take the fight to the now increasingly scarce enemy, the Spitfire wings flew a series of fighter-bomber raids against Sicilian airfields. Beaufighter escorts and general shipping patrols also gained momentum too, and an increasing number of highly vulnerable Axis transport aircraft were also encountered as they attempted to supply armies in North Africa.

No 249 Sqn claimed its first victories of the month on the 11th, when eight Spitfires that were escorting six Beaufighters on an offensive patrol near Pantelleria intercepted a formation of 32 Ju 52/3ms from KGzbV.1, escorted by three Bf 110s and two Ju 88s. All the German aircraft were at sea level, with an unidentified four-engined aircraft above them. The Beaufighters downed five transports, but lost of one of their own, and the Spitfires claimed four Bf 110s (in what was obviously an example of double claiming) and a Ju 88. Amongst those claiming Bf 110s were veteran aces Eric 'Timber' Woods and American Flg Off John J Lynch. This was Lynch's first victory with the unit, but he had previously been credited with two shared kills whilst assigned to No 71 'Eagle' Sqn earlier in the year. In coming months he would emerge as the highest-scoring ace of the post-siege period, and the last great Malta ace.

No 249 Sqn intercepted Ju 88s off Sicily on 13, 14, 17 and 19 December, again whilst escorting Beaufighters, and three were claimed to have been shot down, although the Germans only recorded the loss of two. A pair of Ju 52/3ms were also destroyed by No 1435 Sqn's Flt Lt Bill Walton (in AR561/J-v) on the 17th for his final two kills of the war. These victories elevated him to ace status.

Line abreast, with AR560/JMT nearest the camera, 11 Luqa-based 'Spit-bombers' head for Sicily at low level. This formation represents almost three times the number of Spitfires Malta could put up for air defence in the dark days of March–May 1942. Note that only four of these aircraft are fitted with Vokes air filters. Non-tropicalised Spitfires were shipped to Malta from the late summer of 1942 onwards (*IWM*)

Spitfire VB X-C/serial unknown in early 1943 presents a stark contrast to earlier machines, with its clean finish and general lack of wear and tear. This aircraft could have been one of those thought to have been painted in Royal Navy transport colour Dark Grey Blue. It clearly has light-coloured rounds on the top wing, while the fuselage markings appear to be in standard Roundel Blue. It is thought that with the use of uppersurface colours that were close to Roundel Blue, the roundels were applied in a lighter shade to make them more visible (*via Frederick Galea*)

An American in the RCAF. Flt Lt John J Lynch is seen here in the cockpit of his personal Spitfire VB, EP829. The fighter's score is thought to reflect his tally in late April 1943, Lynch's last victory having been a Ca.313 on the 25th of that month. A few days later, a new victory scoreboard was painted on the panel closest to the cockpit, with *MALTA'S 1,000TH* written in chalk below it for the benefit of a news photographer – see the photograph opposite (*IWM*)

Spitfire VB X-P of No 229 Sqn is shown here at Krendi in early 1943. This aircraft is almost certainly EP606, and it was used by Malta's final ace, Flg Off Leslie Gosling, on 19 April 1943 to claim two Ju 88s from III./KG 76 destroyed northwest of Pantellaria (*via Frederick Galea*)

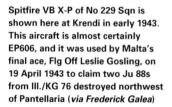

December finished on a celebratory note when the famous Malta reconnaissance pilot Wg Cdr Adrian Warburton made a round trip to Cairo in a repaired Wellington to bring back Christmas spirits for the island's defenders.

A total of 19.5 victories had been scored during December, but the opportunity to gain further kills in the first three months of the new year were few and far between. Indeed, only six victories and a few probables were claimed by the defenders. The first kill in February came on the 7th when Flt Lt John J Lynch (in BR373/T-N) and future ace Flg Off Irving Farmer 'Hap' Kennedy (in EP519/T-C) spotted a Ju 52/3m shortly after they had attacked Gela airfield, on Sicily. Lynch, as the newly appointed 'B' flight commander, made the first pass at the transport, although it had been spotted by Kennedy. He then allowed Kennedy to finish the tri-motor off, thus giving the Canadian his first shared victory.

Another sign of the change of fortunes for Malta's defenders was the arrival of three new Spitfire F IXs for No 126 Sqn in late March. That same month saw just two aerial combats involving defending Spitfire units, the second of which took place on the 25th. Bf 109s from II./JG 27 appeared

over the island unannounced at 0830 hrs, and seven Spitfire Vs from No 229 Sqn and No 126 Sqn's three new Spitfire F IXs were immediately scrambled. Eight of the Messerschmitts were sighted at 22,000 ft, and newcomer Flg Off Ryan Gosling RCAF (in EP606/X-P) of No 229 Sqn gained strikes on one fighter that subsequently crashed. This was his second Malta kill, for he had downed a Z.506B floatplane on 11 February

A year after the first Spitfires had arrived on Malta to secure its defence in the face of a seemingly overwhelming aerial onslaught, the fighter units on the island were now flying uneventful patrols, with little enemy activity in the offing.

To the south, the Axis army in North Africa was in its death throes, despite desperate attempts to rescue it by air. The main job of intercepting these aerial convoys fell to USAAF P-38, P-40 and Commonwealth Kittyhawk units in North Africa, but on occasion Malta's Spitfires did encounter small groups of transports.

Indeed, a number of April's 16 victories took the form of hapless Axis transports, with both 'Hap' Kennedy and now Sqn Ldr J J Lynch hitting their stride during the course of the month. Both men downed two Ju 52/3ms (they were possibly Italian SM.82s) apiece on the 22nd, and more successes were to follow within a few days for Lynch. Having destroyed an Italian Ca.313 on the 25th, the American then garnered significant press attention on 28 April.

During an early morning sweep, Lynch (in EP829/T-N) and Plt Off A F Osbourne spotted two low-flying Ju 52/3ms off the coast of Sicily.

No 249 Sqn CO Sqn Ldr John J Lynch sits in the cockpit of his suitably marked EP829 and admires the handiwork of a chalk-wielding groundcrewman on 28 April 1943 (*via Bruce Robertson*)

Shown here taking centre stage in a *War Pictorial News* film is No 249 Sqn's Sqn Ldr John J Lynch in his personal aircraft EP829/T-N immediately after the sortie in which he scored the 1000th aircraft destroyed by Malta's defences on 28 April 1943. Long thought to have been a tropicalised Spitfire VB, the aircraft was clearly a standard VB with clipped wingtips (*IWM*)

Sqn Ldr Lynch (left) is congratulated by his wingman, Plt Off A F Osbourne, with whom he shared a second Ju 52/3m on 28 April 1943. With the complicity of his unit, the notoriously near-sighted Lynch was often guided to his targets by his wingman. He was carrying out this ruse to avoid being grounded by higher authorities (*IWM*)

Lynch attacked and downed one of the transports, thus assuring his place in the history books as the man who achieved the 1000th kill credited to Malta's defences. He then joined Osbourne in attacking the second Ju 52/3m, which crashed in the sea. Both men subsequently recreated their landing, and Osbourne's congratulations, for the newsreel cameras in a sequence that featured in a *War Pictorial News* film.

Soon after this event, Axis armies surrendered in Tunisia and preparations for the next stage in the Allied offensive began – the invasion of Sicily. The last few months had seen an increase in the American presence in this theatre, and the burden of the offensive against Sicily fell to the USAAF's strategic air forces. Malta's 'Spit-bombers' were no longer needed to strike at Sicilian targets.

As a precursor to the impending changes that were to occur in preparation for the Sicilian invasion, Wg Cdr Wilfred Duncan-Smith arrived to take over the Luqa Wing from Wg Cdr Thompson at the end of May. Duncan-Smith, who was already a 12-kill ace, was to add three more victories to his tally while on Malta.

On 3 July, the Desert Air Force's No 322 Wing arrived from Tunisia, and eventually 23 Spitfire squadrons would be crowded onto Malta prior to the Sicilian invasion. The part that these units played in the capture of Sicily falls outside the scope of this narrative.

'Hap' Kennedy achieved acedom on 10 June when he downed a Bf 109 and shared in the destruction of a C.202 while attached to No 185 Sqn. His unit's job at the time was to interdict Axis supply routes to the eastern Mediterranean, harass German and Italian troops in Sicily, protect Malta from attack and to provide aerial protection to whatever British forces in the area requested their assistance. This included providing air cover for rescue launches and aircraft looking for Allied airmen lost at sea.

Fellow Canadian 'Goose' Gosling also 'made ace' when he downed two Fw 190s on 5 July, taking his tally to six and one shared. He was also the last pilot to achieve ace status flying from Malta. Gosling claimed three more victories on 11 and 12 July, only to be killed in action (along with Sgt W G Downing) fighting Bf 110s during a Catania sweep on 19 July.

In the coming months the war quickly left Malta behind, and No 126 Sqn departed for Italy in September, followed by Nos 249 and 1435 Sqns

Flg Off Irving 'Hap' Kennedy RCAF was one of the late comers to Malta. He eventually became one of only two Malta Spitfire pilots to gain all of their victories in 1943, flying firstly with No 249 Sqn, before being temporarily attached to No 185 Sqn. His last two victories from Malta came on 10 June, and were scored in a Spitfire IX. Subsequently seeing action over Italy, Kennedy finished the war with ten and five shared victories (*via Frederick Galea*)

in October. No 229 Sqn lingered until January 1944, leaving No 185 Sqn as the last of the Malta defenders. It soldiered on alone for months, rarely seeing an enemy aircraft, let alone shooting one down.

Finally, on 22 July 1944, just prior to No 185 Sqn's move to Italy, a Ju 88 was found 90 miles out to sea by Plt Off Ballentine and Lt Rowe. The latter was shot down by the rear gunner, but Ballentine brought the bomber down. After a night at sea, Rowe was rescued by a HSL just in time for a final squadron bash on the 24th, during which the beer flowed freely. The next day No 185 Sqn flew north to Italy.

Flg Off Leslie 'Goose' Gosling RCAF was the very last pilot of the Malta air defence squadrons to become an ace flying from the island. All of his victories were scored in 1943 flying Spitfire VBs with 229 Sqn, his final score being 9.5 kills. On 19 July, Gosling and Sgt W G Downing attacked four Bf 110s over Sicily, and neither pilot returned from this sortie (*via Frederick Galea*)

A mix of tropicalised and non-tropicalised Spitfires from No 229 Sqn taxi out at Qrendi. They are all painted in Dark Blue-Grey camouflage, which was the standard scheme in 1943 (*via Frederick Galea*)

APPENDICES

Spitfire Aces over Malta in 1942

Name	Service	Spitfire Kills over Malta	Total Kills	Squadron/Wing (Malta unit(s) in bold)
Beurling G F	RAF(Canadian)	27.333/0/9	31.333/0/9	403, 41, **249**, 403, 412
Schade P A	RAF	13.5/2/2	13.5/2/2(+3.5 V1s)	**126**, 91
McLeod H W	RCAF	13/2/9.25	21/3/12.25	485, 411, **603, 1435**, 443
Hesselyn R B	RNZAF	12/1/7	21.5/2/7	**249**, 277, 222
Yarra J W	RAAF	12/1/6	12/2/6	**185**, 453
Plagis J A	RAF(Rhodesian)	11/2.75/5.5	15/2.75/6.5	**249, 185**, 64, 126
Weaver C	RCAF(USA)	10.5/3/0	12.5/3/0	**185**, 403
Park N M	RNZAF	10.25/0/1	10.25/0/1	**126**
Brennan V P	RAAF	10/1/6	10/1/6	**249**, 79(RAAF)
Goldsmith A P	RAAF	9.75/2/5	13.75/2/7	242, **126**, 452
Nash P A	RAF	9.5/4.25/2	11.5/5.5/5	609, **249**
Rolls W T E	RAF	8.5/0/1	17.5/3/2	72, 122, **126**
Parkinson C H	RAAF	8.333/3.5/7(+1 on grnd)	8.333/3.5/7(+1 on grnd)	**603, 229**
McElroy J F	RCAF	8/3/10	11.5(+3 postwar)/3/10	**249**, 421, 416, 101(IDFAF)
Tilley R F	RCAF(USA)	8/2/5	8/3/5	121, **601,126**
McNair R W	RCAF	7.75/4/6	16.75/5/14	411, **249**, 411, 421
Woods E N	RAF	7.666/3/7(+1 on grnd)	11.666/4/9(+1 on grnd)	124, 72, **249**, 286 Wing
Jones R O	RAF(USA)	7.833/1/3	7.833/1/3	**126**
MacQueen N C	RAF	7.5/4/4	7.5/4/4	602, **249**
West R	RAF	7.25/3/8.5	7.25/3/8.5	126, **249, 185**
Buchanan G A F	RAF(Rhodesian)	7/3/5	7.5/3/5	41, **249**
Stenborg G	RNZAF	7/0/2	14.333/0/3	111, **185**, 91
Williams J W	RCAF	7/1/11(+1 prob on grnd)	7/1/11(+1 prob on grnd)	**249**
Maclennan I R	RCAF	7/0/8	7/0/8	411, **1435**, 443
Stephens M M	RAF	7/1/3	22/1/5	3, 232, 80, **249, 229, Hal Far Wing**
Smith R I A	RCAF	6.25/0.5/1	13.25/0.5/1	**126**, 412, 401
Grant S B	RAF	6/2.5/6	7/4/6	65, **249, Takali Wing**
Mitchell R A	RAF	6/3/8	6(+6 on grnd)/3/9(+1 on grnd)	**603, 249**, 605
Walton W C	RAF	6/3.5/5	6/3.5/5	**1435**
Bisley J H E	RAAF	5.5/1/0	6.5/1/0	**126**, 452
Varey A W	RAF	5.5/4/7	5.75/4/7	**126**, 66
Johnson W J	RAF	5.58/5/2	6.58/5/2	145, **126**
Dodd W G	RCAF	5.333/2/4	6.666/3/4	**185**, 402
Ballantyne J H	RCAF	5.25/1/7	5.25/1/7	**603, 229**, 403
Reid D G	RCAF	5/3/4.5	5/3/4.5	**185**
Evans K W S	RAF	5/3/3	5/3/3	600, 130, **126**, 165
Scott A H	RAF	5/2/5	6/2/5	124, **603, 1435**, 122
Jones F E	RCAF	5/0/2	5/0/3	72, **249**

Spitfire Aces over Malta in 1943

Name	Service	Spitfire Kills over Malta	Total Kills	Squadron (Malta unit(s) in bold)
Lynch J J	RCAF(USA)	12.5/1/1.5	13.5/1/1.5	71, **249**
Gosling L C	RCAF	9.5/0/3	9.5/0/4	222, **229**
Kennedy I F	RCAF	5.25/0/0	12.25/1/0	**249, att 185**,111, 93, 401

Spitfire Aces with at least one confirmed victory over Malta

Name	Service	Spitfire Kill(s) over Malta	Total Kills	Squadron/Wing (Malta unit(s) in bold)
Barnham D	RAF	4.5/1/1	5.5/1/1	609, **601**
Barton A R H	RAF	1/3.5/7	6/3.5/9	32, **126**
Bisdee J D	RAF	2/1/0	9/4/3.5	609, **601**
Charney K L	RAF	3/3/5	6/4/7	**185**, 602, 132
Curry J H	RCAF(USA)	1/0/0	7.333/2/3	**601**
Daddo-Langlois W R	RAF	4.5/0/2	5.5/0/2	**249**, 93
Dicks-Sherwood E S	RAF(Rhodesian)	4.5/0/4.5	6/0/5.5	266, **603, 229**, 92
Douglas W A	RAF	3/1.5/4	6/2.5/7	**603**, 453, 611
Duncan-Smith W G G	RAF	3/1/1	18/7/8	611, 603, 411, 64, North Weald Wing, **Luqa Wing**, 244 Wing, 324 Wing
Hanks P P	RAF	4/2/5	13/1.333(+2 on grnd)/6	1, 257, Coltishall Wing, **Luqa Wing**
Hibbert W J	RAF	1/0/1	5/0/2(+2 on grnd)	**126**, 124, 274
Hurst J	RAF	3.5/2/3.5	4.5/7/4.5	**603**
Ingram M R B	RNZAF	2/0/0	10.5/3/5	611, **601**, 243, 152
Johnston H A S	RAF	2/5/2	5.25/5/2.5	257, 133, **126**, 165, 65
Lovell A D J	RAF	4.75(+1 on grnd)/0/6.666	18.25(+1 on grnd)/2/10.5	41, 145, **1435**, 322 Wing
Northcott G W	RCAF	1.5/1/3.5	8.5/1/7.5	401, **603, 229**, 402, 126 Wing
Peck J E	RAF(USA)	3.5/3/9	4.5/3/10	**126**, 2nd FS/52nd FG(USAAF)
Rae J D	RNZAF	4.5/3.5/4	12/8.5/6	485, **249**, 485
Reid L S	RAAF	4/1/6	4/1/6	130, **185**, 79(RAAF)
Thompson J M	RAF	2/0.5/2	8/1.5/7	111, **Hal Far Wing**

Confirmed Spitfire Victories by Malta Air Defence Squadrons, March 1942 to May 1943

Squadron	249	126	601	603	185	1435	229	Wing Commanders	Totals
1942									
March	14.5	6							20.5
April	37	13	2.5	3.25					55.75
May	31	27.25	11	19.25	12.5				101
June	15	9	7	3	17				51
July	44	46.75	to Egypt	15.25	33.5	2.5			142
August	3	7		Disbanded and absorbed by 229	10	13	4		37
September	3.666	3			3	1	-	0.333	10.999
October	41	41.5			11	22	19.5	9.5	144.5
November	-	2			1	2	-	-	5
December	12	1			-	4	1	1.5	19.5
Totals	**201.166**	**156.5**	**20.5**	**40.75**	**88**	**44.5**	**24.5**	**11.333**	**587.249**
1943									
January	-	1			-	-	-	-	1
February	1	-			-	-	1	-	2
March	2	-			-	-	-	1	3
April	9	1			1	0.5	4.5	-	16
May	4	1			-	-	3	-	8
Totals	**16**	**3**			**1**	**0.5**	**8.5**	**1**	**30**
Grand Totals	**217.166**	**159.5**	**20.5**	**40.75**	**89**	**45**	**33**	**12.333**	**617.249**

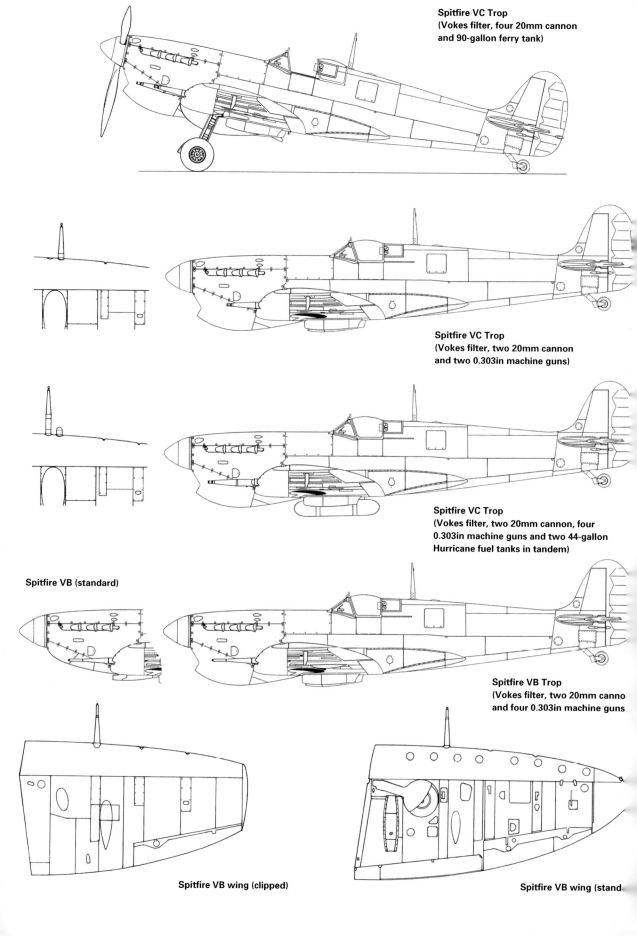

Spitfire VC Trop
(Vokes filter, four 20mm cannon
and 90-gallon ferry tank)

Spitfire VC Trop
(Vokes filter, two 20mm cannon
and two 0.303in machine guns)

Spitfire VC Trop
(Vokes filter, two 20mm cannon, four
0.303in machine guns and two 44-gallon
Hurricane fuel tanks in tandem)

Spitfire VB (standard)

Spitfire VB Trop
(Vokes filter, two 20mm canno
and four 0.303in machine guns

Spitfire VB wing (clipped)

Spitfire VB wing (stand

All drawings on this page are
of a **Spitfire VC**, and they are
to 1/72nd scale

COLOUR PLATES COMMENTARY

1

Spitfire VB AB264/GN-H of Plt Off Peter Nash and Flt Lt Robert McNair, No 249 Sqn, Takali, March 1942

AB264 was amongst the first batch of 15 Spitfires flown into Malta, and it wore standard desert colours of Middle Stone and Dark Earth, but with Sky Blue undersides substituted for Azure Blue. Sky Blue was best described as a light powder blue, and not at all like standard Sky. Indeed, it was very similar to Luftwaffe RLM 76. On landing in Malta, the March batch of Spitfires were reportedly repainted dark grey (presumably Extra Dark Sea Grey), with white codes and serial numbers – the Sky Blue was left untouched. On 26 March, future ace Flt Lt Buck McNair claimed a third of a kill flying AB264 when he was involved in the downing of a Ju 88 from I./KG 54. He also lodged claims for a Ju 87 and Ju 88 probably destroyed and another Ju 88 damaged. AB264 had a long career on Malta, eventually ending up with No 1435 Sqn in October as Z-v. It was overhauled and passed on to the USAAF in May 1943.

2

Spitfire VB AB451/GN-T of Flg Off George Buchanan, No 249 Sqn, Takali, 1 April 1942

One of seven Spitfires sent to Malta as part of Operation *Picket I* on 21 March 1942, AB451 was flown by Rhodesian ace Flg Off 'Buck' Buchanan on 1 April when five Spitfires were sent to intercept Ju 87s, Ju 88s and Bf 109s headed for Grand Harbour and Hal Far. He was credited with a Ju 87 probable and a Bf 109 damaged following this sortie.

3

Spitfire VC BP964/1-X of Sgt Adrian Goldsmith RAAF, No 126 Sqn, Luqa, April 1942

BP964 was *Calendar* Spitfire VC, with standard tropicalisation and four cannon. This aircraft was reportedly re-camouflaged with paint acquired from the ship's store – probably US Navy Blue-Grey. When newly applied, this paint was fairly dark, but it tended to fade drastically with exposure to the elements. It was also very likely that other paints were used, and mixed to stretch the available supply. A No 601 Sqn machine, the aircraft had the code '1' applied in place of the unit's usual 'UF' two-letter code. BP964 was used by Sgt Adrian Goldsmith to down a Bf 109 on 21 April, and Sqn Ldr John Bisdee got a Ju 88 with it later that same day. Flt Lt Bill Douglas was flying BP964 when he claimed a share in the destruction of a Ju 87 during the 10 May aerial battles, and he then downed a Bf 109 with it the following day. The aircraft received serious battle damage on 13 May and was struck off charge, having flown just 18.25 hours since it was built two months earlier.

4

Spitfire VC BP962/2-R of Flt Lt William Douglas, No 603 Sqn, Takali, April 1942

Another four-cannon *Calendar* Spitfire, BP962 was marked with a '2' in place of No 603 Sqn's usual 'XT' code letters. Veteran Flight Leader Flt Lt Bill Douglas downed a Ju 88 in this aircraft during a large raid by more than 80 Luftwaffe bombers on 25 April. Douglas, who already had one kill from operations over France with No 603 Sqn in 1941, went on to claim two

more victories over Malta, followed by a pair over the Normandy invasion beaches in June 1944 whilst flying a Spitfire VB with No 611 Sqn. This took his final wartime tally to six. BP962's career was nowhere near as long as Bill Douglas', however, for the aircraft was destroyed on 1 May 1942 when shot down with New Zealander Flt Sgt Jack Rae at the controls. Rae survived, and later scored 4.5 victories over Malta. He ended the war with a score of 11 and 2 shared kills.

5

Spitfire VC BR190/2-A of Flt Sgt Paul Brennan RAAF, No 249 Sqn, Takali, April–May 1942

Flt Sgt Brennan used BR190 to down a Bf 109 south of Gozo on 4 May for his sixth victory. By this time the aircraft had had two of its 20-mm cannon removed, leaving it with the standard Spitfire VC armament of two 20-mm weapons and four 0.303-in machine guns. The finish of its Dark Blue-Grey uppersurface scheme had the look of being both roughly and hastily applied, and it was very thin, or non-existent, around the fuselage roundels and code-letters. Note that the Blue-Grey was applied to BR190 with the distinctive US Navy wraparound on the leading edge of the wings. This aircraft was also struck off charge on 13 May, having flown just 13.20 hours.

6

Spitfire VC BR195/1-Q of Plt Off Peter Nash, No 249 Sqn, Takali, 16 May 1942

One of the first Spitfire pilots to 'make ace' on Malta, Plt Off Peter Nash scored a shared victory over a Bf 109 with Plt Off 'Johnny' Plagis (in BR176) whilst flying BR195 on 16 May. This was No 249 Sqn's 100th Malta victory. The following day, Nash used BR195 to down a Bf 109, but he was shot down and killed by another Messerschmitt fighter several hours later. His final score was 11.5/5.5/5. A *Calendar* Spitfire, BR195 was highly unusual in having what appeared to be Azure Blue undersurfaces instead of the more typical Sky Blue.

7

Spitfire VC serial unknown/U of Flt Lt Denis Barnham, No 601 Sqn, Luqa, 14 May 1942

This Spitfire was used by Flt Lt Denis Barnham on 14 May to down a Ju 88 from KGr 806, having shared in the destruction of a Junkers bomber with Plt Off Bruce Ingram minutes earlier. Despite there being at least four photographs of this aircraft, its serial remains unrecorded. This is the famous machine that featured white spots near its uppersurface wingtips, and which also had its canopy briefly removed. The aircraft featured a four-cannon armament and faded Blue-Grey uppersurfaces. Barnham, who had been an artist pre-war, flew into Malta from *Wasp* in Operation *Calendar*. Already credited with an Fw 190 destroyed over the Channel front with No 609 Sqn, he added one Italian and three and one shared German aircraft to his tally with No 601 Sqn. He saw no more action after Malta.

8

Spitfire VC BP975/1-K of Flt Lt Denis Barnham, No 601 Sqn, Luqa, 24 April 1942

BP975 was a typical *Calendar* Spitfire camouflaged with either

US Navy Blue-Grey paint or a mixed blue drawn from ship's stores. There was much inconsistency in the application of this paint, which was applied with everything from paint brushes to mops. Many of the Spitfires featured a wraparound of the uppersurface colour over the leading edge of the wing, which remained in vogue with the US Navy throughout the war. Flt Lt Denis Barnham was flying this aircraft when he downed a Stuka on 24 April, this aircraft being one of 14 Ju 87s and 34 Ju 88s that had targeted Malta's fighter airfields late in the day. BP975 subsequently served with No 249 Sqn as T-T from July 1942 until it was passed on to the USAAF on 31 August 1943.

9

Spitfire VC BR107/C-22 of Plt Off Peter Nash, No 249 Sqn, Takali, May 1942

BR107 is one of the 'mysterious' C/number-coded Spitfires, and this profile is based purely on conjecture. These fighters were thought to have been flown off *Eagle* as part of Operations *Calendar* and *LB*. Although photos of dark-painted Spitfires on *Eagle* exist from around this time, none are seen wearing C/number codes. These aircraft were in the thick of the crucial May air battles on the 9th, 10th and 14th, and their appearance represents a still outstanding missing link from the campaign. BR107 was struck off charge on 5 Februay 1943.

10

Spitfire VC BR126/3-X of Plt Off Jerry Smith RCAF, No 126 Sqn, Luqa, 9 May 1942

This was the Spitfire that famously landed on USS *Wasp* after it had suffered a malfunction with its 90-gallon slipper tank. Typical of the *Bowery* Spitfires, it appeared to be painted in a lighter shade of blue than the *Calendar* Spitfires. The *Bowery* fighters had had their Desert colours overpainted at Gibraltar, and it appears that this job was done using spray guns, with a feathered edge between the top and bottom colours. Most had the uppersurface camouflage extended to the bottom of the Vokes filter, leaving only its undersurface in Sky Blue. Following brief service with No 126 Sqn, BR126 joined No 185 Sqn, where it wore the code letters GL-O. Pilots flying the fighter downed two Bf 109s, and it survived a belly landing on 15 June only to be destroyed in a bombing raid on 31 July.

11

Spitfire VC BR187/2-G of Flt Lt William Douglas, No 603 Sqn, Takali, 3 May 1942

BR187 was a typical No 603 Sqn *Calendar* Spitfire, featuring a *Wasp* overpaint, but with the Desert colours left around the serial number. It was used by Flt Lt William Douglas to damage a Bf 109 on 3 May, but the fighter was written off in a crash-landing by Sgt J W Connell of No 601 Sqn the very next day.

12

Spitfire VC BR290/1-T of Sgt Adrian Goldsmith RAAF, No 126 Sqn, Luqa, 14 May 1942

Sgt Goldsmith was credited with downing a Bf 109, a Ju 88 and a Z.1007 in this aircraft on 14 May. BR290 was a *Calendar* Spitfire, which was photographed still wearing its 1-T delivery code some six months after it had arrived on Malta. Like several other Malta Spitfires it had no underwing roundels, and its cannon were mounted in the outboard position on each wing, with only a single 0.303-in machine gun inboard. This armament arrangement may have been unique to Malta-based Spitfire VCs. This aircraft moved to Sicily with the unit on 1 August 1943 and was struck off charge on 30 September.

13

Spitfire VC BR294/GL-E of Sgt Wilbert Dodd RCAF, No 185 Sqn, Hal Far, 22 May 1942

Flt Sgts Don Reid and Wilbert Dodd both achieved successes with BR294 in the spring of 1942, the latter having flown the fighter to Malta from *Eagle* on 29 March. Leaving the island with 5.333 victories to his name, he had raised his total to 6.666 by war's end. With BR294, Dodd added Bf 109s to his score on 22 May and 6 July (two kills on the latter date). Don 'Shorty' Reid claimed two Bf 109s destroyed in this aircraft on 1 and 2 July, but BR294 was badly damaged in this action and struck off charge the following day. A *Bowery* Spitfire, it carried No 185 Sqn's distinctive yellow codes, which stood out in stark contrast against the fighters' Blue-Grey background.

14

Spitfire VC BR349/3-C of Sgt Tony Boyd RAAF, No 185 Sqn, Hal Far, 14 May 1942

Sgt John Livingstone Boyd's only Spitfire victory was achieved in BR349/3-C on 14 May 1942, when he downed the Bf 109F flown by Leutnant Alfred Hammer of 4./JG 53. He was killed in this aircraft a few hours later whilst dogfighting with C.202s and Re.2001s. Flying into Malta from HMS *Ark Royal* in November 1941, Boyd had claimed all of his early victories (four and two shared) flying Hurricane IIs with Nos 242 and 185 Sqns. BR349 was typical of the *Bowery* machines, and again their exact colour match up is pure speculation. What is known is that these Spitfires were almost certainly painted en route, as photos exist showing them in what appears to be standard factory Desert camouflage on board *Wasp*, but then repainted in Blue-Grey by the time they departed the carrier.

15

Spitfire VC BR246/B of Plt Off Frank Jones RCAF, No 249 Sqn, Takali, 6 June 1942

Plt Off Frank Jones scored a shared victory whilst flying this aircraft when he and Flg Off Raoul Daddo-Langlois downed a Ju 88 from KüFlGr 66 on 6 June. Minutes later Jones claimed his second kill when he destroyed an Re.2001. This aircraft was reportedly wearing the delivery code C-40 when it arrived on Malta during Operation *Style* on 3 June, and the Spitfire was subsequently re-coded T-J in the summer. By the time BR246 was sent to the central Mediterranean, Spitfires were being painted at Gibraltar in preparation for service on Malta. Its dark uppersurfaces suggest that it had been repainted in either Dark Mediterranean Blue, Extra Dark Sea Grey or even Light Mediterranean Blue, which was actually quite dark. Mediterranean Blues were the best colours to use, but supplies were limited in 1942. There are reports that paint was thinned so much on Malta that the end product suffered from poor adhesion, allowing bleed-through of underlying colours. Mixing different shades was also common practice. BR246 was lost on operations on 13 August 1942.

16

Spitfire VC serial unknown/UF-M of Plt Off Bruce Ingram RNZAF, No 601 Sqn, Luqa, 15 June 1942

UF-M was famously shown taking off in the wartime newsreel 'Malta G.C.' to cover the *Vigorous* convoy. Spitfires covering this convoy were fitted with two torpedo-shaped Hurricane long-range tanks under the fuselage. On 15 June, while flying UF-M, Kiwi Plt Off Bruce Ingram was credited with the destruction of a Ju 87 southeast of Pantellaria, this kill being shared with squadronmate Sgt Allen-Rowlandson.

17

Spitfire VC BR321/GL-J of Flt Lt 'Johnny' Plagis, No 185 Sqn, Hal Far, 6–7 June 1942

Although this aircraft was the personal mount of 'Johnny' Plagis, it was flown by several other pilots from No 185 Sqn prior to being lost on 2 August 1942. Ioannis Agorastos Plagis was born in Hartley, Southern Rhodesia, to Greek parents. Volunteering for the RAF, he was sent to the UK for training in the spring of 1941. He was quickly christened 'Johnny' upon his arrival in England, and the name stuck for the rest of his life. Upon the completion of his training (he was classed as being above average in all his flying assessments), Plagis was posted to No 65 Sqn in late June 1941, but moved to No 266 Sqn the following month. Receiving orders for the Middle East in January 1942, he flew a Spitfire off *Eagle* into Malta on 6 March during Operation *Spotter*. Assigned to newly reformed No 249 Sqn, Plagis became the first Spitfire ace of the Malta siege on 1 April when he claimed four victories (he had scored his first kill on 25 March). On 3 June he was posted to No 185 Sqn as 'B' flight commander, and three days later he claimed two Re.2001s destroyed in BR321. A Bf 109 followed 24 hours later, and this proved to be Plagis' final Malta victory. On 7 July he was despatched by way of Gibraltar back to the UK, where he was found to be suffering from malnutrition, scabies and fatigue. Once restored to health, and following a spell as an instructor, he joined No 64 Sqn as a flight commander, scoring two more victories. Plagis then took command of the reformed No 126 Sqn in July 1944, and claimed a further two kills flying Spitfire IXs over the Normandy invasion beaches, prior to converting to Mustangs and flying bomber escort missions.

18

Spitfire VC BR387/GL-W of Plt Off John 'Slim' Yarra RAAF, No 185 Sqn, Hal Far, July 1942

BR387 was the personal aircraft of Jack 'Slim' Yarra, who joined the RAAF in October 1940. He trained in Canada, before being sent to the UK and joining No 232 Sqn in October 1941. He had moved to No 64 Sqn within two weeks, however, and in February 1942 he received orders sending him to Malta. Yarra was present at the first two attempts to launch Spitfires to the embattled island from *Eagle*, but was chosen as a spare pilot and had to wait until 21 March to fly off with the second group of aircraft (at the controls of AB333). Upon his arrival on Malta, he was initially assigned to No 249 Sqn, although he was subsequently transferred to No 185 Sqn, which was short of Hurricane pilots at the time. On 9 May more Spitfires arrived, and No 185 Sqn began receiving them, although the Hurricanes lingered on for a while. Yarra quickly achieved success over the island, and five of his 12 Malta kills came at the controls of BR387 between 21 June and 7 July. This machine was subsequently passed on to the Free French Air Force in May 1944, and eventually struck off charge in July 1945.

19

Spitfire VB BR562/X-R of Flt Lt Ray Hesselyn RNZAF, No 249 Sqn, Takali, July 1942

Ray Hesselyn flew off *Eagle* on 7 March 1942 and landed at Takali, whereupon he joined No 249 Sqn. His first victory did not come until 1 April, when he destroyed a Ju 87 and a Bf 109. Although he was himself shot down on 20 April, Hesselyn continued to enjoy success in the air. He and BR562 came together in the final days of his tour on Malta, and he claimed his last two of 12 kills with it on 8 July (a Bf 109 and a Ju 88, with a second bomber damaged). In July 1943 Hesselyn joined No 222 Sqn on the Channel front, and he claimed 6.5 kills with the unit between 17 August and 3 October. On the latter date he was shot down in flames moments after destroying three Bf 109Gs, which took his tally to 21.5 victories. Wounded in both legs, Hesselyn spent the rest of the war as a PoW. BR562 was lost on operations on 18 January 1943.

20

Spitfire VC BR295/T-H of Plt Off Lawrence Verrall RNZAF, No 249 Sqn, Takali, 27 June 1942

BR295 was one of several Spitfires on Malta that had the blue proportions of its fin flash and upper wing roundels painted in a lighter shade, presumably to contrast with the Dark Mediterranean Blue or mixed Dark Blue-Greys that were prevalent on Malta Spitfires. Its finish was rather rough, with odds bits of the original camouflage either not covered or showing through. Kiwi Verall downed an Re.2001 with BR295 on 27 June, this success being his third, and last, kill on Malta. This aircraft was lost in combat on 18 July.

21

Spitfire VC BP989/4-N of Flg Off Wally McLeod RCAF, No 603 Sqn, Takali, 9 July 1942

BP989/4-N is representative of the *Bowery* Spitfires, some of which seem to have been painted a lighter tone than the *Calendar* Spitfires. McLeod, who was the leading RCAF ace on Malta with 13 kills, claimed a Bf 109F damaged on 5 July and a Ju 88 probably destroyed four days later whilst flying BP989. The fighter was lost on operations on 16 October.

22

Spitfire VC serial unknown/N-MK of Flt Sgt 'Paddy' Schade, No 126 Sqn, Luqa, 9 July 1942

Second-ranking Malta ace Flt Sgt 'Paddy' Schade used N-MK to down two Bf 109s on 9 July, these claims taking his tally at that time to 12.5 kills. This Spitfire had very dark uppersurfaces that are thought to be have been Dark Mediterranean Blue, with Sky Blue undersides. It also sported No 126 Sqn's new MK code letters that had been introduced in June.

23

Spitfire VC BR130/T-D of Sgt George Beurling, No 249 Sqn, Takali, 14 July 1942

Despite being the focal point of probably the most famous Malta Spitfire photograph (seen on page 56), little is known about the actual career of BR130. Sgt George Beurling crash-landed BR130 after being slightly wounded in the heel by shrapnel from an explosive bullet on 14 July, and on 14 October Wg Cdr Arthur Donaldson damaged a Ju 88 with the fighter (by then coded T-S). The latter pilot was in turn seriously wounded by an accurate burst of fire from an escorting Bf 109 just minutes later, forcing him to crash-land BR130 at Takali. The fighter was eventually passed on to the USAAF at the end of October 1943. BR130 boasted a number of features peculiar to Malta Spitfires. Being a *Calendar* aircraft, it was resprayed with US Navy Blue-Grey or a mixed Blue-Grey paint prior to reaching Malta. The fighter also featured the uppersurface wraparound on the leading edge of the wing that was almost unique to Blue-Grey Spitfires. Yet another Malta trademark was the retention of one cannon in the outer wing position and one machine gun inboard. BR130 also had fuselage roundels with a late-war style reduced yellow outline. The rudder and lower cowling panels were finished in desert camouflage, and the uppersurface paint was badly worn in general.

24
Spitfire VC BP952/F-MK of Plt Off Rod Smith RCAF, No 126 Sqn, Luqa, July 1942
Brothers Jerry and Rod Smith both enjoyed aerial success with BP952, the fomer downing a Ju 88 on 10 July and damaging a Junkers bomber 16 days later. On 18 July younger brother Rod was flying as wingman to Jerry (who was in BR175/Q-MK) when the pair probably destroyed a Ju 88 north of Malta. BP952 was lost on operations on 17 November.

25
Spitfire VB EN976/T-C of Plt Off John McElroy RCAF, No 249 Sqn, Takali, July 1942
EN976 was one of the first Spitfire VBs sent to Malta, the aircraft being assigned to No 249 Sqn in July 1942 – it was lost on operations on 25 August. Plt Off John McElroy was posted to Malta in June, flying off *Eagle* on 9 June in Operation *Salient* – he damaged the tailwheel of his Spitfire on take-off, causing him to crash upon landing in Malta. A steady scorer of victories between early July (on 23 July, flying EN976, he claimed a share in a probable Bf 109 kill and damaged a second German fighter) and late October, McElroy's tally stood at eight kills, three probables and ten damaged by the time he completed his tour in December. McElroy returned to operations on the Channel front as a flight commander with No 421 Sqn RCAF in January 1944, and gained two kills with the unit soon after D-Day. Assuming command of No 416 Sqn in July 1944, he had claimed an additional 1.5 kills by war's end. McElroy's postwar career took an interesting turn when, in 1948, he volunteered for service with the fledgling Israeli Defence Force Air Force, again flying Spitfire IXs. He scored three kills in 1948–49 – an Egyptian C.205 and two RAF Spitfire FR 18s. Fellow Canadian ace Plt Off John Williams claimed two Bf 109 kills on 27 July flying EN976.

26
Spitfire VC BP869/T-K of Sgt Vasseure Wynn RCAF, No 249 Sqn, Takali, 28 July 1942
BP869 was one of the Operation *LB* Spitfires that flew in to Malta on 19 May. By July it was sporting typical No 249 Sqn markings. Note that this aircraft still boasts an early-war roundel. The transition from early- to late-war roundels on the island seems to have started with the arrival of the Operation *Pinpoint* Spitfire VBs in early July, and this change was made on aircraft already on Malta as time permitted over subsequent months. As late as 9 September, there were still examples of

early wartime roundels and fin flashes, as seen on BR112/X of No 185 Sqn. American Sgt Vasseure Wynn, who was known on Malta as 'Georgia' despite coming from Oklahoma, was flying BP869 when he damaged a Bf 109 on 28 July. RCAF ace Flt Lt Frank Jones downed a Bf 109 in the fighter on 8 August.

27
Spitfire VC BR301/UF-S of Plt Off John McElroy RCAF, No 249 Sqn, Takali, July 1942
BR301 was probably the single most successful Spitfire on Malta, being an ace in its own right. A *Bowery* aircraft, it wore badly faded Blue-Grey camouflage, with large sections of its undersurface colour scheme (Dark Earth and Middle Stone) showing though on the rear fuselage and spine. It was also fitted with two cannons in the outboard position and only two machine guns inboard, and it also had no underwing roundels. McElroy claimed 2.5 kills in this aircraft between 7 and 13 July and Sgt Beurling downed four on 27 July and one two days later. A further 1.5 kills were credited to other pilots whilst flying BR301. The fighter was damaged on 27 July and struck off charge two days later, having flown 54.20 eventful hours.

28
Spitfire VC BR375/GL-A of Plt Off Gray Stenborg RNZAF, No 185 Sqn, Hal Far, June 1942
Kiwi ace Plt Off Gray Stenborg was one of several pilots to enjoy success with veteran Spitfire BR375, claiming a Bf 109 destroyed (to 'make ace') and two Ju 88s damaged whilst flying it on 15 July. A veteran of previous combat on the Channel front with No 111 Sqn, Stenborg had achieved seven victories by the time he left Malta in late August. Posted to Spitfire XII-equipped No 91 Sqn in the summer of 1943 as a flight commander, he claimed an additional 3.333 victories prior to being killed in action on 24 September. BR375 was also used by ace Plt Off Ken Charney to down the first Bf 109G-2 credited to a Malta Spitfire on 5 September 1942. The fighter survived additional service in North Africa and the Middle East, and was struck off charge in August 1945.

29
Spitfire VB EP200/GL-T of Flt Sgt Colin Parkinson RAAF, No 603 Sqn, Takali, July 1942
EP200 landed on Malta as part of Operation *Insect* on 21 July, this aircraft being one of the earliest examples of a Spitfire VB sent to the island. Its uppersurfaces appear to be have been overpainted with mixed Blue-Grey or possibly Extra Dark Sea Grey paint. Note too that although the fighter's GL code letters have been applied in their usual shade of yellow, its individual letter T is in white. Australian ace Flt Sgt Colin Parkinson scored a probable Bf 109 kill in EP200 on 14 July, and followed this up with a confirmed Bf 109 victory on the 15th. Plt Off J W Guthrie was credited with a Ju 88 destroyed in EP200, but this was the last success for the fighter, as on 27 August American pilot Flg Off P A Woodger crash-landed on a Sicilian beach after the aircraft had been hit in the engine by Italian AA fire.

30
Spitfire VB EP706/T-L of Plt Off George Beurling, No 249 Sqn, Takali, October 1942
This Spitfire was marked up with George Beurling's ever growing victory tally beneath its cockpit, and he used it to

down four Bf 109s in late September and early October. During the 'October *Blitz*', he scored all six of his victories (his last on Malta) in BR173/T-D. EP706 was subsequently passed on to the USAAF in January 1944, and was eventually scrapped in August 1946.

31

Spitfire VC BR112/X of Sgt Claude Weaver RCAF, No 185 Sqn, Hal Far, 9 September 1942

American Sgt Claude Weaver flew a Spitfire VB off *Eagle* to Malta on 15 July. Posted to No 185 Sqn at Hal Far, he found himself in the thick of the action almost immediately, downing a Bf 109 on the 17th, two more Messerschmitts on the 22nd and then another pair of German fighters on the 23rd. Weaver claimed a share in a Ju 88 on the 24th, giving him three straight days of success – these victories were all scored in EP122. On 31 July he was shot down (in EP343) by ranking Luftwaffe Malta ace Oberleutnant Gerhard Michalski of II./JG 53. Having achieved four more victories in August, Weaver was brought down by a C.202 whilst in pursuit of another Macchi fighter during a sweep over Sicily on 9 September – he had destroyed an Italian fighter just a few minutes earlier. His crash-landed Spitfire BR112/X was subsequently photographed by the Italians on the beach at Scoglitti.

32

Spitfire VB EP691/X-A of Plt Off Colin Parkinson RAAF, No 229 Sqn, Takali, October 1942

EP691 well illustrates the wear and tear inflicted on Malta Spitfires. It is thought to have been flown into Malta on 17 August as part of Operation *Baritone*. Plt Off Parkinson enjoyed notable success with this aircraft between 11 and 13 October, claiming one kill, three probables (one shared) and a damaged. EP691 was lost on operations on 23 January 1943.

33

Spitfire VB EP717/D-v of Flt Sgt Ian Maclennan RCAF, No 1435 Sqn, Luqa, 11 October 1942

Flown to Malta on 6 September, EP717 features the standard markings of No 1435 Sqn – the only RAF squadron with a four-digit number. Like Nos 229 and 249 Sqns at this time, its aircraft wore just a one-letter ID code. No 1435 Sqn's V code was applied in a smaller size than the individual aircraft letter, and always aft of the roundel. Seven-kill ace Flt Sgt Ian Maclennan claimed two Ju 88s destroyed and a third one damaged in this aircraft on 11 October. This machine was struck off charge on 4 March 1943.

34

Spitfire VC BR311/L-MK of Flt Lt William Johnson, No 126 Sqn, Takali, July 1942

BR311 appears to have arrived on Malta as part of Operation *Salient*, possibly still wearing desert camouflage. As this profile shows, its MK code letters were painted on by hand askew. Ace Flt Lt William Johnson claimed his last two kills (a pair of Re.2001s) in this aircraft on 14 August whilst providing fighter protection for the Operation *Pedestal* convoy. Ten-kill ace Sgt Nigel Park also enjoyed success with BR311, claiming three Ju 88s destroyed in it on 12 October. Thirteen days later, having just achieved his tenth victory, Park was shot down and killed in this very machine.

35

Spitfire VC BR379/T-V of Sgt Tommy Parks, No 249 Sqn, Takali, July 1942

Although records are vague, BR379 probably arrived on Malta during Operation *Style*, and survived until it was shot down on 4 October by a Bf 109 whilst being piloted by Flt Sgt G A Hogarth, who was killed. During the fighter's brief career on Malta, it was flown by two notable non-aces in No 249 Sqn, namely Sgt Thurne 'Tommy' Parks (who destroyed a Bf 109 and damaged a second one with BR379 on 2 July) and Flg Off Norman Lee. The latter piilot's only confirmed victory came on 6 July over a C.202, and it was scored in BR379 – his total score was one destroyed, two and two probables and nine and one shared damaged. Lee's high number of probable and damaged claims demonstrates the dire conditions of combat over Malta, where pilots simply could not wait around to try to confirm a kill if they expected to live to fight another day.

36

Spitfire VC AR560/JM-T of Wg Cdr John Thompson, Luqa Wing, Luqa, April 1943

Wg Cdr Thompson was already an ace by the time he reached Malta with new AOC AVM Keith Park in mid-July 1942. Instrumental in helping the latter implement new tactics for the interception of Axis raids, he led both the Takali and Hal Far Wings, adding a Bf 109 and a Ju 88 to his tally, along with several probables and damaged claims. Thompson flew AR560 throughout the spring of 1943, by which point he had taken over the Luqa Wing, and was regularly leading it on 'Spit-bomber' raids over Sicily. This aircraft was lost on operations on 29 June 1943.

37

Spitfire VC BR498/PP-H of Wg Cdr Peter Prosser Hanks, Luqa Wing, Luqa, October 1942

This aircraft saw much action in the 'October *Blitz*', with Wg Cdr Hanks claiming four kills, three damaged and two probable ground victories in it. Flt Lt Bill Rolls also claimed five victories in the aircraft during the same period. BR498 was similar to an increasing number of Spitfires reaching the island in the autumn of 1942 in that it had no tropical air filter fitted in an effort to improve the fighter's performance. With nine kills to its credit, BR498 tied with BR301 for the title of the highest scoring Spitfire on Malta. Surviving the war, the fighter was struck off charge on 13 September 1945.

38

Spitfire VB EP829/T-N of Sqn Ldr John J Lynch RCAF, No 249 Sqn, Krendi, April 1943

Another high-scoring Malta Spitfire, EP829 was used by American ace Sqn Ldr John J Lynch to inflict a heavy toll on Axis transports attempting to fly supplies to Tunisia in April 1943. Claiming five and one shared kills during this month, Lynch's most publicised victory came on 28 April, when he downed the 1000th enemy aircraft (a Ju 52/3m) credited to the defenders of Malta. Ironically, this aircraft was passed on to the Italian Air Force postwar.

39

Spitfire VB AB535/T-Z of Flg Off 'Hap' Kennedy RCAF, No 249 Sqn, Krendi, April 1943

On 22 April 1943, Flg Off 'Hap' Kennedy, flying AB535/T-Z, and Sqn Ldr John J Lynch in EP829, downed four 'Ju 52/3ms' (these aircraft were possibly Italian SM.82s) off the coast of Sicily. Both pilots claimed two aircraft apiece. Six days later Plt Off A F Osbourne (in AB535/T-Z) supported Sdn Ldr Lynch when he scored Malta's 1000th kill. Osbourne, who had spotted the transports, shared the destruction of a second Ju 52/3m with his CO. AB535 was written off in a flying accident on 6 February 1944.

40

Spitfire VB EP606/X-P of Flg Off Ryan Gosling RCAF, No 229 Sqn, Krendi, April 1943

By the spring of 1943, No 229 Sqn's Spitfires were mostly painted in faded Dark Earth and Extra Dark Sea Grey, with Azure Blue undersides. EP606 was used by ace Flg Off Leslie Gosling to down a Ju 88, and share in the destruction of another Junkers bomber with Sgt A J Clayton, on 19 April 1943. This fighter was eventually passed on to the French Air Force postwar.

─── ACKNOWLEDGEMENTS ───

The author would like to thank Frederick Galea of the Malta Aviation Museum Foundation for his help in providing images and accompanying information for this volume. Thanks also to the staff of the film and photographic archives of the Imperial War Museum, as well as Douglas Radcliffe MBE and Andrew Renwick of the Royal Air Force Museum. Other friends and fellow enthusiasts have also generously provided material and support, notably Brian Cull, Philip Kaplan, Barrett Tillman, Tim Addis, Paul Lucas, Neil Robinson, Graham Boak, Patrick Lee, Michael Percival, George Mellinger, Edward Bejes, William Ostrander, Chris Walton, William Pryor, Joe Testa, Mike Aube, Doug Povirk, Allan Zimmerman, Joanne King and Wallis Nichols.

─── AUTHOR'S NOTE ───

In 1992, a handful of aviation enthusiasts, ably led by Ray Polidano, joined forces to reconstruct to static condition the surviving wreckage of Spitfire IX EN199, which had been found in a Maltese scrap yard. The project, completed in time for public display on the occasion of the 50th anniversary of VE-Day in May 1995, led to the formation of the Malta Aviation Museum Foundation, with its principle aim of setting up an aviation museum in Malta. Slowly, this project started to materialise, and today the Foundation has acquired premises at Takali (Ta' Qali), with two Romney Huts on site, and has since, with the help of European Union funding, erected a new hangar that houses its World War 2 aircraft. A small but growing number of machines have been collected, some in need of restoration. As the Foundation is a purely voluntary body, progress cannot be rapid owing mainly to a lack of funds. Local and overseas membership is encouraged, and a quarterly newsletter is published. More can be learned about the Foundation's activities at its website – www.maltaaviationmuseum.com

─── BIBLIOGRAPHY ───

Barnham, Denis, *One Man's Window.* William Kimber, 1956
Beurling, George & Roberts, Leslie, *Malta Spitfire.* Greenhill Military Paperbacks, 1973
Brennan, Paul, Hesselyn, Ray & Bateson, Henry, *Spitfires over Malta.* Jarrolds Publishers London Ltd, 1943
Caruana, Richard J, *Victory in the Air.* Modelaid International Publications, 1996
Cull, Brian, *249 at War.* Grub Street, 1997
Cull, Brian & Galea, Frederick, *Spitfires over Malta.* Grub Street, 2005
Cull, Brian & Malizia, Nicola with Galea, Frederick, *Spitfires over Sicily.* Grub Street, 2001
Douglas-Hamilton, David Lord, *The Air Battle for Malta.* Airlife, 1981
Franks, Norman, *Buck McNair – Canadian Spitfire Ace.* Grub Street, 2001
Halley, James, *Squadrons of the RAF & Commonwealth.* Air Britain, 1968
Halliday, Hugh, *The Tumbling Sky.* Canada's Wings, 1978
Hamlin, John F, *Military Aviation in Malta G.C. 1915–1993.* GMS Enterprises, 1994
Haugland, Vern, *The Eagles' War.* Aronson, 1982
Jefford, Wg Cdr C G, *The Eagle Squadrons.* Ziff-Davis Flying Books, 1979
Johnston, Tim, *Tattered Battlements.* William Kimber, 1943 and 1985
Kennedy, I F, *Black Crosses off my Wingtip.* General Store Publishing House, 1994
Lucas, 'Laddie', *Malta – The Thorn in Rommel's Side.* Stanley Paul & Co, 1992
McAulay, Lex, *Against All Odds.* Hutchinson Australia, 1989
McCaffrey, Dan, *Hell Island.* James Lorimer & Co Ltd, 1998
Morgan, Eric B & Shacklady, Edward, *Spitfire – The History.* Key Publishing Ltd, 1998
Nolan, Brian, *Hero.* Lester & Orpen Dennys Ltd, 1981
Olnyk, Frank, *Stars & Bars.* Grub Street, 1995
Price, Alfred, *Spitfire at War I.* Charles Scribners & Sons, 1974
Price, Alfred, *Spitfire at War 2.* Ian Allan Ltd, 1985
Price, Alfred, *Spitfire at War 3.* Ian Allan Ltd, 1990
Rae, Jack, *Kiwi Spitfire Ace.* Grub St, 2001
Rogers, Anthony, *185 – The Malta Squadron.* Spellmount Limited, 2005
Rawlings, John D R, *Fighter Squadrons of the RAF.* MacDonald, 1969
Rolls, W T, *Spitfire Attack.* William Kimber, 1987
Ross, David with Blanche, Bruce & Simpson, Robert, *The Greatest Squadron of Them All Vol 2.* Grub Sreet, 2003
Shores, Christopher, *Aces High Vol 2,* Grub Street, 1999
Shores, Christopher, *Those Other Eagles.* Grub Street, 2004
Shores, Christopher & Cull, Brian with Malizia, Nicola, *Malta – The Spitfire Year 1942.* Grub Street, 1991
Shores, Christopher & Williams, Clive, *Aces High Vol 1.* Grub Street, 1994
Shores, Christopher, Ring, Hans & Hess, William, *Fighters over Tunisia.* Neville Spearman, 1974

INDEX

References to illustrations are shown in **bold**. Plates are shown with page and caption locators in brackets.